Social work and multi-agency working

Making a difference

Edited by KATE MORRIS

BASW
BRITISH ASSOCIATION
OF SOCIAL WORKERS

First published in Great Britain in 2008 by

The Policy Press
University of Bristol
Fourth Floor
Beacon House
Queen's Road
Bristol BS8 1QU
UK

Tel +44 (0)117 331 4054
Fax +44 (0)117 331 4093
e-mail tpp-info@bristol.ac.uk
www.policypress.org.uk

British Library Cataloguing in Publication Data
A catalogue record for this book is available from the British Library.

Library of Congress Cataloging-in-Publication Data
A catalog record for this book has been requested.

ISBN 978 1 86134 945 3 paperback
ISBN 978 1 86134 946 0 hardcover

Cover design by The Policy Press.
Front cover: image kindly supplied by www.JohnBirdsall.co.uk
Printed and bound in Great Britain by Henry Ling Ltd, Dorchester.

For my Dad – Selwyn Morris

SOCIAL WORK IN PRACTICE series

Series editors: Viviene Cree, University of Edinburgh and **Steve Myers**, University of Salford

"This new series combines all the elements needed for a sound basis in 21st century UK social work. Readers will gain a leading edge on the critical features of contemporary practice. It provides thoughtful and challenging reading for all, whether beginning students or experienced practitioners." **Jan Fook**, Professor in Social Work Studies, University of Southampton

This important series sets new standards in introducing social workers to the ideas, values and knowledge base necessary for professional practice. Reflecting the current curricula of the new social work degree and post-qualifying programmes and structured around the National Occupational Standards, these core texts are designed for students undertaking professional training at all levels as well as fulfilling the needs of qualified staff seeking to update their skills or move into new areas of practice.

Editorial advisory board:
Suzy Braye, Sussex University
Jill Manthorpe, King's College London
Kate Morris, University of Birmingham
Lyn Nock, BASW
Joan Orme, Glasgow University
Alison Shaw, The Policy Press

Titles in the series:
Social work: Making a difference by Viviene Cree and Steve Myers
Social work and multi-agency working: Making a difference
 edited by Kate Morris
Youth justice in practice: Making a difference by Bill Whyte
Social work and people with learning difficulties: Making a difference
 by Susan Hunter
Radical social work in the 21st century: Making a difference
 by Iain Ferguson and Rona Woodward

Contents

Acknowledgements

Thanks go to the late Jo Campling for all her support – her advice and robust guidance is sorely missed. I would also like to thank all the contributors to this text; they provided me with chapters that made the task of editing remarkably straightforward. Special mention should be made of Tony Glynn, one of the co-authors of the chapter looking at mental health. Tony died before this text was published – his contribution to social work learning was invaluable and he is greatly missed. The series editors provided me with useful advice and feedback, and helped with the task of editing. Thanks also to staff at The Policy Press, and to Sara Kinahan for her unscrambling of the drafts! Finally thanks go to my family for their tolerance, support and patience.

Notes on contributors

Apostol Apostolov is a Research Fellow in the Department of Education at the University of Oxford. His areas of research include inter-agency work, innovations in the third sector, and multicultural education. He also has strong links with international practitioner communities.

Jane Coad is a Senior Research Fellow in the Centre for Child and Adolescent Health at the University of the West of England, Bristol, and is an Honorary Senior Research Fellow at the University of Birmingham. Using her background in art and nursing, Jane undertakes participatory research in child health and across a range of health and social care settings. Jane works on projects in both Bristol and the West Midlands, and at a national level currently this includes work for 'Action for Sick Children' and the Department of Health.

Alex Davis is a registered social worker who has had 25 years' experience of working in mental health services. He is a member of Suresearch, a network of mental health service users and their allies involved in teaching and research. He is a co-author of 'Claiming DLA; an information pack for adults up to age 65 using mental health services, their carers and advocates'.

Ann Davis is Professor of Social Work and Director of the Centre of Excellence in Interdisciplinary Mental Health at the University of Birmingham. Ann's research interests include user experiences of services, poverty and mental health. Her most recent publication is *Social Work: Voices from the Inside*, which she wrote with Viviene Cree. Ann is a member of Suresearch, a network of mental health service users and their allies involved in teaching and research.

Irene Dooher qualified as a social worker in 1969 and has extensive experience as a local authority social worker. She has also had planning roles in relation to adult mental health/learning difficulties and children's services. She helped to establish the Leicester Children's Fund and the local children's trust arrangements. Her current specialism is in Child and Adult Mental Health Service (CAMHS) developments, including commissioning and performance managing these services.

Anne Edwards is Professor of Education in the Department of Education at the University of Oxford. She was Director of the National Evaluation of the Children's Fund (NECF) and is Co-Director of two Economic and Social Research Council (ESRC) studies that are looking at the impact of interprofessional work in preventing the social exclusion of children in the practices of the workers involved. She has written extensively on learning in the professions and how practitioners work with disadvantaged groups.

Sarah Galvani is an Associate Professor in the School of Health and Social Studies at the University of Warwick. Her practice background pre- and post-qualifying spans work with people with mental ill-health, homelessness, alcohol and drug problems, HIV and domestic abuse. Her main research interests are the links between substance use and domestic abuse and how social workers are prepared for and address substance use among their service users. She is currently a trustee of Aquarius, a Midlands-based alcohol and drug charity.

Tony Glynn was a User Involvement Co-ordinator at the Centre of Excellence in Interdisciplinary Mental Health, University of Birmingham. He had over 20 years' experience of using mental health services and was a member of Suresearch, a network of mental health service users and their allies involved in teaching and research. His most recent publication, *Two Decades of Change: Celebrating User Involvement,* co-authored with Marion Clark, was published in 2007.

Nathan Hughes is Lecturer in Social Policy and Social Work in the Institute of Applied Social Studies at the University of Birmingham. His teaching and research interests include social and political discourses regarding young people, and associated policy and practice, particularly in relation to crime and anti-social behaviour.

Leonie Jordan is a solicitor who has worked with families and child welfare professionals in statutory agencies, private practice and the voluntary sector. She has undertaken policy and research work and is interested in developing socio-legal knowledge and skills in partnership with the social care workforce.

Rosemary Littlechild is a Senior Lecturer in Social Work in the Institute of Applied Social Studies at the University of Birmingham. Her research and publication interests are in work with older people, community care, partnership working between social care and health services and service user and carer involvement.

Kate Morris is currently Head of Social Work at the University of Birmingham. She previously managed the National Evaluation of the Children's Fund, a large-scale multidisciplinary research project commissioned by the Department for Education and Skills. She is a qualified social worker and her research and teaching interests are in participation, prevention, family involvement in child welfare and the evaluation of innovative child welfare practices.

Anna Popova is a Research Officer, working for the Learning in and for Inter-agency Work project at the University of Bath. Her major interests include personal and professional development, teacher education and training, special needs education and international education. Her doctoral thesis is about transformations in pedagogic practices in Russia with a particular focus on cultural and historical exploration of activities.

David Prior is a Senior Research Fellow in the Institute for Applied Social Studies at the University of Birmingham. His main research interests are in community safety and anti-social behaviour and their links to citizenship and governance. Before joining the Institute he had over 20 years' experience of partnership working in local government, in contexts including health and social care, crime and disorder reduction, urban regeneration and neighbourhood renewal.

Nicki Ward is a Lecturer in Social Work in the Institute of Applied Social Studies at the University of Birmingham. Her teaching and research interests include social work values and ethics; equality, diversity and social identity; advocacy and empowerment; and qualitative research methodology. Before becoming a lecturer Nicki worked for 25 years with people with learning difficulties in a variety of statutory, voluntary and not-for-profit organisations.

Setting the scene

Kate Morris

Introduction

A dominant characteristic of contemporary policy and practice across the range of social care activity is the emergence of multi-agency working. While historically this may have been often held at the point of strategic development, most recently there has been a shift towards collaborative working and the co-location of provision and practice development at the point of delivery. For some areas of social care the trend towards multi-agency working is becoming established (in mental health and youth justice for example); in other areas it is still relatively underdeveloped. Research shows that effective multi-agency working is a skilful and challenging activity, involving considerable demands at both practice and policy levels. Those using services describe multi-agency working as enhancing service provision when done well, and as frustrating and disempowering when delivered ineffectively (FPA, 2005). Collaborative working is being explored in various settings and is the focus of a growing body of research and evaluation reports (see, for example, Warmington et al, 2005; Edwards et al, 2006).

This introductory text brings together a range of disciplines and authors to consider the issues and challenges involved in multi-agency working for social work practice. The aim is to offer an informed introduction to policy, practice and research surrounding multi-agency working, and to ensure that messages for social work practice learning and development are identified. This text is unusual in drawing together contributors from different disciplines. This multidiscipline approach reflects the theme of the book, and enables the reader to gain insights into a range of social care settings and to consider a range of professional and user reflections on social work practice.

Given the diverse professional backgrounds, each contributor presents a different perspective on the role of social work in the service area they consider. It is this challenge of different discourses that runs as a theme throughout the text.

This opening chapter serves as a short overview of the text and provides some guidance on the aims and uses of this book. The chapter briefly considers the use of a multitude of terms within the text and their implications. The context for practice is outlined, but it should be noted that each chapter offers an overview of the relevant legal and policy context. Finally, a short summary of each contribution is provided.

This text primarily explores the policy and practice issues within England, although some reference is made by some contributors to developments in Wales and Scotland. However, the themes emerging from the England-focused contributions are relevant to broader developments nationally (where similar multi-agency working developments are under way) and internationally.

Defining the terms

The contributors to this text use a number of terms to capture the process of different disciplines and professions coming together to plan and deliver services. Within the chapters there are examples of the following interpretations:

■ multi-agency working as a process of arriving at some shared strategic goals but with single agency activity within the overarching plans (Galvani; Jordan);

■ multi-agency working as a process involving collective goals for service provision but with independent execution of the various tasks and activities by each professional at the point of service delivery (Edwards et al; Ward);

■ multi-agency working as a shared process of both planning and direct delivery of services with co-location of staff and services (Hughes and Prior).

As Edwards (2004) argues elsewhere, understanding how different terms are being utilised is crucial and often reveals the practices that are being developed. The use of 'collaborative working' may or may not describe co-location of staff and shared practices. Equally 'multi-agency working' may reflect in reality (as Galvani suggests in Chapter Seven) only nominal joint agency activity.

In exploring the dimensions of joint working this text does not use a prescribed definition for multi-agency working or the associated terms adopted by the different contributors. Part of the challenge for social work practice illustrated by the different chapters is in the diversity of terms and understandings. Imposing external definitions on these perspectives would lead to significant differences being masked. Instead, the range of understandings described offers useful learning for those seeking to develop multi-agency practices. However, using the learning from the chapters, the conclusion offers some ways forward in terms of understanding the different terms and their implications for practice.

The context for practice

The fact that a diverse group of contributors could be drawn together to discuss social work in a context of multi-agency working indicates the growing prevalence of expectations for multi-agency working. As the chapters in this text illustrate, the changing landscape for social work practice means that there are few settings for social work where some form of joint agency activity is not a requirement for effective provision and practice. Legal and policy requirements now formalise expectations for 'joined-up' provision (see, for example, the 2004 Children Act; DH, 2006). As a result, the contested concept of partnership runs as a theme through the levels of multi-agency working – strategic, operational and at the point of delivery and take-up. The debates about the conceptual understandings of partnership working and the reality as experienced by those using the services reveal the extent to which tensions between political decisions and professional identities can emerge. The political and policy discourses of partnership can be seen to reveal a complex process of change in governance and service provision (Glendinning, 2002; Sullivan and Skelcher, 2002). In this text, contributors also struggle with the implications and realities of this conceptual framework – and in some settings it is argued that there is little evidence of partnership working beyond some strategic intent. The boundaried nature of professional identities and agency cultures is repeatedly cited in the contributions as a barrier to the intended integrated arrangements (Coad; Edwards et al; Littlechild).

These contextual policy changes have provoked a series of debates within social work both nationally and internationally. The recent consultations by the General Social Care Council (GSCC) in 2006 on the role and identity of social work are in part a response to this changing context. This process spelt out what were judged to be the defining characteristics of social work, and how social work can support and work within interprofessional settings. The role of social work within interprofessional working was a key theme, alongside that of service user involvement and influence. Some multi-agency working rests heavily on the role of social work – as Jordan describes in Chapter Five. Social work in this setting – child protection – is seen as being central to the processes of enabling safe outcomes for children. However, the changing legal, policy and practice expectations also raise tensions for social work. These can be seen to cluster either around the pressures on social work to develop new skills and practices, as Hughes and Prior describe in Chapter Two, or around a crucial role for social work in influencing and changing the environment for practice, as Edwards et al explore in Chapter Four.

There are also concerns about the valuing of the profession and its identity when set within an environment where other professions are perceived to be well established and clearly defined. The moves to bring together health and social care raise particular challenges for social work (Glasby and Peck, 2004) and both Coad and Littlechild, in Chapters Three and Nine, set out some of the tensions and challenges. The fast-moving context for social work practice is particularly evident in the changing structures for social care and health services, where there may be embedded health-based models for practice that clash with those used by social work, and Coad in Chapter Three highlights the tensions that may arise.

Social work education and training

A statement produced by the International Federation of Social Work (IFSW, 2000) seeks to bring together the knowledge and purpose of social work:

> The social work profession promotes social change, problem solving in human relationships and the empowerment and liberation of people to enhance well-being. Utilising theories of human behaviour and social systems, social work intervenes at the points where people interact with their environments. Principles of human rights and social justice are fundamental to social work.

Throughout the IFSW statement little reference is made to multi-agency working or to locating social work within a broader picture of associated disciplines and professions. The extent to which multi-agency working is a focus of attention and concern internationally is uneven; however, it is evident that within the UK, as a result of significant policy developments, social work has begun seriously to address the skills and learning needed for multi-agency working. The core requirements for social work education and training make clear these expectations alongside the strategic developments in social care training.

Department of Health requirements for the social work degree state that 'Partnership working and information sharing across professional disciplines and agencies' is one of the key areas for assessed learning and development (DH, 2002, p 4). The range of requirements and expectations suggests that qualifying and post-qualifying social workers must begin to consider how best to work collaboratively. However, as the chapters in this book illustrate, broader changes in organisational structures and professional boundaries may be necessary for social work to be able to fully support and promote multi-agency working.

Most recently the concept of integrated training has emerged, with agencies such as the Children's Workforce Development Council (CWDC) exploring how different professionals may begin to learn together. However, as the contributors to this text suggest, while shared training may offer many positives, it also brings with it some complex debates about values and ethical frameworks. Such debates may be assisted by the production of assorted training packs and toolkits to support this activity (DfES, 2003) but the issues raised within this book indicate that conceptual and theoretical developments are also required.

Some of the chapters place a particular emphasis on the experiences of those using the services (for example, Chapters Five and Six). The extent to which service users are able to participate in multi-agency strategic and operational developments is patchy, despite the policy expectations for such involvement. Unease has been expressed about the debates surrounding multi-agency working being preoccupied with interprofessional relationships to the detriment of service user involvement (Morris, 2004). Littlechild explores this issue in Chapter Nine, as does Ward in Chapter Eight, and it is also picked up within the concluding chapter. The experience of the most marginalised of families – who face particular barriers because of ethnicity, culture or identity – indicates that they are particularly at risk of being absent from commissioning and planning processes. The evidence indicates that the focus of concern is problem led and is often upon the excluded rather than the excluding, and within this rich and varied community models of social empowerment and care are ignored (Barnes et al, 2006; Morris et al, 2006). The experiences of marginalised families and communities are reflected in the contributions to this text, but are also picked up and further considered in the concluding chapter.

A guide to this book

This book serves as an introduction to the complex themes of multi-agency working. Each chapter sets out the legal and policy context as it relates to the particular set of needs being considered, and where possible there is also some analysis of the level and types of needs that services are seeking to meet. The chapters describe the challenges and opportunities presented by multi-agency working and draw out some of the key messages for social work. The chapters offer illustrative practice material and some trigger questions to enable the reader to apply the learning to their professional development.

Youth justice has an increasingly distinct professional identity – drawing on elements from a range of disciplines including social work, youth work, the police and community safety. Recent legal and policy frameworks make clear the requirement for multi-agency and multiprofessional delivery of services. Hughes and Prior consider in Chapter Two the expectations for youth justice services to be developed collaboratively, and they explore the extent to which this has played out in reality. They identify the challenges for the development of effective services and within this the messages for social work practice.

The bringing together of health and child welfare services gained impetus with the National Service Framework (DH, 2004) and the expectation of the Change for Children Agenda (DfES, 2004). In Chapter Three Coad considers how these services are currently taking multi-agency working forward, and some of the barriers and opportunities that are emerging. She locates the experiences of children within this context and sets out how children might influence the development of services. The messages both for social work learning and development and for joint agency activity are identified.

The joining up of education and social services departments with the roll-out of the 2004 Children Act and its associated guidance raises significant challenges for multi-agency development. In Chapter Four Edwards et al use the example of an extended school provision to tease out the broader messages for multi-agency working from an education perspective. Drawing on empirical data, the chapter is able to describe the current boundaries and tensions in multi-agency working in educational settings. The messages for social work are examined, as are the broader messages for professional development and learning.

In Chapter Five Jordan describes the experiences of those using social care services and the messages that emerge for multi-agency working. She examines and captures the perspective of families who need to, or have to, take up child welfare provision. In particular she considers how child protection services are delivered, and how families would want to see multi-agency provision developed. Jordan, and the families she quotes, articulate the frustrations and opportunities experienced when needs and problems require a range of agencies to work together.

Jordan's chapter draws heavily on the narratives of service users – a theme that is reflected in Chapter Six. This chapter is co-written by a mental health service user and examines how multi-agency working has developed within the context of mental health services.

While the needs and experiences of those with drug and alcohol problems cross the boundaries of traditional professional territories, as Galvani explores in Chapter Seven, the capacity of agencies to collaborate can vary significantly. Galvani describes some of the policy and professional barriers to multi-agency working, identifies how these might be addressed and, within this, describes the messages for social work.

In the context of learning disability, multi-agency working has an uneven history. In Chapter Eight Ward explores the evolution of multi-agency working in providing services to adults with learning disabilities. She considers how social work has traditionally contributed to this area and how it might develop to better respond to the needs of those using the services and the requirements for effective multi-agency working.

Littlechild in Chapter Nine considers how multi-agency working has developed in the delivery of services to older people. She reflects on the needs and wishes of those using the services and explores how professional collaboration has more or less responded to these needs. The role of social work, in a sphere increasingly linked into healthcare, is described and key principles for effective practice are set out.

The concluding chapter (Chapter Ten) explores a series of key themes that arise from the contributions. The chapter considers whether operational definitions for the plethora of terms for multi-agency working can be arrived at, and the implications these definitions might have for practice. The role and influence of those using social work services is considered – and particular attention is paid to the experiences of black and minority ethnic families. Finally, through locating the discussion in a wider international context, the next steps for social work education and training are explored – and the key messages summarised.

The diverse professional backgrounds of the authors of the chapters inform their contributions. The contributors include those with backgrounds in health (Coad), law (Jordan), education (Edwards), social work (Galvani, Littlechild and Ward) and policy development and service use (Davis, Glynn and Prior). There is a growing body of social work literature that describes from the viewpoint of social work the challenges and opportunities of 'joined-up' working (Quinney, 2006). This text captures an analysis of the learning necessary for social work from the perspective of those charged with working alongside social workers in developing and supporting multi-agency working.

References

Barnes, M., Evans, R., Plumridge, G. and McCabe, A. (2006) *Preventative Services for Disabled Children: A Final Report of the National Evaluation of the Children's Fund*, London: DfES.

DfES (Department for Education and Skills) (2004) *Every Child Matters: Change for Children*, London: DfES.

DH (Department of Health) (2002) *Requirements for Social Work Training*, London: DH.

DH (2004) *The National Service Framework for Children, Young People and Maternity Services*, London: HMSO.

DH (2006) *Our Health, Our Care, Our Say: A New Direction for Community Services*, London: HMSO.

Edwards, A. (2004) *Multi-agency Working for Prevention for Children and Families: 'It's the Biggest Change since the Introduction of the NHS'*, www.ne-cf.org

Edwards, A., Barnes, M., Plewis, I. and Morris, K. (2006) *Working to Prevent the Social Exclusion of Children and Young People: Final Lessons from the National Evaluation of the Children's Fund*, RR 734, London: DfES.

Family Policy Alliance (2005) *Supporting Children and Families*, Briefing Paper, London: Family Rights Group.

Glasby, J. and Peck, E. (2004) *Care Trusts: Partnership Working in Action*, Abingdon: Radcliffe Publishing.

Glendinning, C., Powell, M. and Rummery, K. (2002) (eds) *Partnerships, New Labour and the Governance of Welfare*, Bristol: The Policy Press.

IFSW (International Federation of Social Workers) (2000) *Definition of Social Work* (www.ifsw.org/en), last accessed January 2008.

Morris, K. (2004) 'Partnership working: changing understandings in child welfare services in England', *Protecting Children*, vol, 19, no 2, pp 61–8.

Morris, K., Warren, S., Plumridge, G. and Hek, R. (2006*) Preventative Services for Black and Minority Ethnic Children: A Final Report of the National Evaluation of the Children's Fund*, London: DfES.

Quinney, A. (2006) *Collaborative Social Work Practice*, Exeter: Learning Matters.

Sullivan, H. and Skelcher, C. (2002) *Working Across Boundaries: Collaboration in Public Services*, Basingstoke: Palgrave Macmillan.

Warmington, P., Daniels, H., Edwards, A., Leadbetter, J., Martin, D., Brown, S. and Middleton, D. (2005) *Interagency Collaboration: A Review of the Literature*, Bath: Learning in and for Interagency Working project.

2

Delivering youth justice through partnership working

Nathan Hughes and David Prior

Introduction

The history of official responses to the perceived problem of offending by young people is characterised by continuing struggles between competing value positions and knowledge claims; for instance, between understandings of the young person as 'deprived' or 'delinquent' and between prescriptions for discipline, rehabilitation or social support as means of dealing with such young people (see Muncie, 1999). Social work has been, and remains, at the heart of such struggles. In this chapter we sketch the current value orientation, policy context and core organisational arrangements through which 'youth justice' is pursued, highlighting both the implications for social workers and the significance of 'partnership' in the current system. We then examine how partnership working is seen as contributing to effective practice across different dimensions of service delivery, development and management. A key aim is to identify both the opportunities and the challenges for social workers that are apparent in this attempt to deliver youth justice through partnership.

BOX 2.1: *Glossary of terms used*	
ASBO	Anti-social Behaviour Order
ASSET	Assessment process developed by the YJB for use by YOTs
CAMHS	Child and Adolescent Mental Health Services
EPQA	Effective Practice Quality Assurance
ISSP	Intensive Supervision and Surveillance Programmes
KEEP	Key Elements of Effective Practice
KIQ	Key Indicators of Quality
MAPPA	Multi-agency Public Protection Arrangements
YJB	Youth Justice Board
YOT	Youth Offending Team

The 'problem' of youth crime

Providing an accurate account of the nature and extent of youth crime is notoriously difficult (Bateman, 2006). Statistics are available in relation to 'detected' crime, that is, crime committed by young people that is reported to and recorded by the police; but this constitutes only a very small proportion of the total number of offences that young people themselves acknowledge, through self-report surveys, as having committed. Moreover, as we shall see below, the youth justice system is concerned not just with criminal offences, but with forms of 'anti-social behaviour' that are not crimes and therefore not recorded as part of the official youth crime statistics. Even more problematically, much activity within the youth justice system is geared towards young people judged to be 'at risk' of involvement in crime, aiming to prevent offending that has not yet occurred and is therefore not measurable. Bearing all this in mind, the following statistics give some sense of the scope of youth offending for the year 2004 (Nacro, 2006):

- 112,900 indictable offences were committed by young people under 18 years – a drop of 21% from the total for 1992.
- The number of 15- to 17-year-old males who were cautioned, reprimanded or warned for an indictable offence was 5,479 for every 100,000 of the population – compared to 7,065 in 1992.
- 63% of indictable offences by young people were property-related – only 17% of offences involved some form of violence against the person.
- Among those surveyed, 35% of boys and 22% of girls aged 10–17 years admitted to at least one of 20 core offences (although many of these were relatively minor).

The legal and policy context

Reform of the system for responding to youth crime in England and Wales was a major priority for the New Labour government elected in 1997. During the government's first year in office, six separate consultation papers were published, leading to the White Paper *No More Excuses* (Home Office, 1997) setting out proposals for significant changes in the policy and legal framework for dealing with young offenders and those thought likely to become offenders. This was rapidly followed by the passing of the 1998 Crime and Disorder Act, which incorporated many of those changes and established, in effect, a completely new youth justice system. Subsequent legislation has reinforced and extended the system introduced in 1998 (see Box 2.2).

The characteristics of the 'new youth justice' that have particular significance for social workers can be examined under five main headings: policy and strategy; organisational arrangements; management processes; practices and services; and knowledge base (Prior, 2005).

Policy and strategy

In relation to policy and strategy, the fundamental change enacted by the new legislation was to establish a single overriding objective for the whole of the youth justice system: 'to prevent offending by children and young persons' (1998 Crime and Disorder Act, section 37). This marked a clear break with past strategies for dealing with young people who got into trouble with the law (Muncie, 1999; Pitts, 2001). The focus was not on responding to the developmental or other needs of young people, as had characterised the 'welfare' approach to young offenders to which social work made a

BOX 2.2: *Summary of key legislation*	
1998 Crime and Disorder Act	Prevention of offending defined as core objective of youth justice system Established Youth Justice Board (YJB) and Youth Offending Teams (YOTs) Legal concept of 'anti-social behaviour' introduced with associated sanctions (ASBOs) Provisions for control of the under-10s Parenting Orders introduced Replacement of police cautions with formal system of Reprimands and Final Warnings
1999 Youth Justice and Criminal Evidence Act	Elements of 'restorative justice' introduced – Referral Orders and Youth Offender Panels
2002 Police Reform Act	Introduced Interim ASBOs, which could be obtained in an emergency
2003 Criminal Justice Act	Introduced Individual Support Orders to accompany ASBOs imposed on young people
2003 Anti-Social Behaviour Act	Extended powers for dealing with anti-social behaviour, including mechanisms for enforcing parental responsibility in relation to children who behave anti-socially; powers for police to disperse groups in designated areas; powers to close premises where drugs are used unlawfully ('crack house closures')

key contribution. Nor was it principally on diverting young people away from the criminal justice system, thus avoiding exposure to the damaging impacts that could result from that. It was not even geared towards concerns that young offenders should be punished in appropriate ways (although a punitive strain of thought clearly ran through many of the new proposals). Rather, the new strategy focused directly on young people's behaviour and specifically on preventing certain forms of behaviour. The prevention of youth offending became the core purpose that helped shape the organisation and delivery of the whole new approach (Newburn, 2002).

The revised policy framework also contained other features that had implications for the way social workers and other practitioners related to children, young people and their families. In particular it began to obscure the traditional distinction between young people's behaviour that was criminal, and therefore dealt with through the criminal justice system, and behaviour that, although it might be problematic, was non-criminal and so dealt with by other services such as childcare, education or health. Thus the 1998 Act introduced the legal concept of 'anti-social behaviour' to refer to behaviour that did not constitute a criminal offence but was seen as causing harm to others, and established a range of legal sanctions to control such behaviour. Young people whose behaviour gave cause for concern and who would once have been responded to by welfare agencies were thereby brought into the operations of the criminal justice system (Squires and Stephen, 2005). A further blurring of the criminal/non-criminal distinction resulted from measures introduced in the 1998 Act that allowed children below the age of criminal responsibility (10 years), who were thus legally incapable of committing crimes, to be placed under court-imposed Child Safety Orders to control their behaviour (Bandalli, 2000). These orders may require the child to be supervised by a social worker, but it is supervision in the context of a criminal justice, not a childcare framework. Finally, the new system generated an expansion of the idea of responsibility in relation to young people's behaviour, with parents liable to be subjected to legal sanctions as a result of anti-social or criminal behaviour by their children (Drakeford and McCarthy, 2000).

Organisational arrangements

The key innovation in the organisational arrangements associated with the new youth justice system was the emphasis on multi-agency or partnership-based structures. The partnership principle was especially apparent at the local level in the creation of YOTs in every local authority area, with team members drawn from a range of different agencies, services and professions. Thus many social workers transferred into the new teams and became redesignated as 'YOT workers' alongside other staff from different professional backgrounds (Dugmore and Pickford, 2006).

Management processes

As regards management processes, at a national strategic and coordinating level the YJB was created to provide oversight, direction, resourcing and monitoring of the new system. The YJB sets performance targets for YOTs, holding them accountable for effective delivery of planned service outputs within allocated budgets (Newburn, 2002).

Practices and services

Further innovation was apparent in relation to developments in practices and services, with many new services, programmes and initiatives established, either through forms of sentences made available for young offenders, with specified programmes of work attached to them, or as preventive initiatives addressing young people deemed to be 'at risk' of becoming involved in offending behaviour. Such initiatives were often designed to target particular groups, such as persistent young offenders, young offenders with drug-related problems or young people exposed to risks because of where they lived. These practice developments thus operated in quite different contexts: conventional criminal justice settings such as youth custody or community penalties, new approaches to responding to young offenders such as restorative justice techniques, and social programmes addressing the impact of multiple deprivation on young people.

Knowledge base

The knowledge base underpinning the whole approach was regarded as especially important, in line with the government's general insistence that policy and practice should be 'evidence led'. Initiatives and programmes developed and implemented within the new youth justice system were to be grounded in reliable evidence, derived from systematic research, about 'what works' (Prior, 2005). The implication was that only those forms of practice that could be demonstrated to be effective in preventing youth offending would be countenanced within the new system.

The kinds of changes outlined above were significant not only in creating a new system for responding to youth crime, but in bringing concerns about young people's offending and anti-social behaviour into the mainstream of policy and practice in relation to services for children and young people generally. Subsequent policy developments such as the Green Paper *Every Child Matters* (DfES, 2003), *Youth Justice: Next Steps* (Home Office, 2003), the 2004 Children Act, the Green Paper *Youth Matters* (DfES, 2005) and the *Respect Action Plan* (Respect Task Force, 2006) chart an increasing emphasis on 'inter-agency governance', and the 'integration' of strategies, processes and service delivery in order to achieve 'interdependent outcomes'; a process demonstrated most strongly with the creation of children's trust arrangements to bring together all local services for children and young people (DfES, 2004). Achieving reductions in offending by young people thus became an objective for the whole network of child- and youth-related services; and partnership working between agencies and professionals therefore became a paramount requirement.

YOTs: partnerships at the heart of the new youth justice

The most significant of such partnership-based developments was the establishment of the local YOTs under section 39 of the 1998 Crime and Disorder Act. This set out a clear multi-agency framework for the creation of YOTs, in which the local authority would be the lead agency but with the required cooperation of police services and health authorities. Each YOT was to include, as a minimum, a local authority social worker, a police officer, a probation officer, a health service worker and a representative of the local education authority; others could also be recruited according to local needs and circumstances. The core tasks of YOTs were to coordinate the provision of youth justice services and to deliver the local youth justice plan (which local authorities were required to produce).

Research evaluating the implementation and early experiences of the new arrangements suggested that YOTs had succeeded in establishing themselves as operational partnerships relatively quickly and had begun to develop a distinctive ethos and style of working, successfully 'melding the skills and expertise of members from different agencies' (Holdaway et al, 2001, p 113). Other research, however, indicated that the speed of implementation meant that practitioners in the new YOTs kept largely to forms of practice with which they were already familiar (Bailey and Williams, 2000, p 83), suggesting that the 'melding' of skills and expertise still had some way to go. Smith (2003) comments on this tendency for professional roles within YOTs to remain distinct and for specialisms to be preserved: for example, the YOT police officer being the 'victim specialist' because this area of expertise was carried over from the police service (p 106) or the social worker specialising in family relationship issues (p 114). Although it may seem to undermine the idea of an integrated multidisciplinary team, this continuing specialisation can have advantages, as when the social worker is able to call on the wider resources of their 'parent' agency to help address a particular situation (Smith, 2003).

Questions about how the principles of multi-agency working were played out in practice within YOTs were explored in a detailed study of one English YOT (Burnett and Appleton, 2004). An issue of central significance to the team's development was whether YOT practitioners should aim to be generic and multiskilled or would be more effective by preserving their individual expertise and specialisms – whether the partnership should resemble a 'fruit salad', in which ingredients retained their individual qualities, or a 'fruit cake', in which the ingredients were transformed into a uniform whole (Burnett and Appleton, 2004, p 37). The researchers identified numerous examples of the benefits of different forms of knowledge and practice being brought together, with much mutual learning and appreciation of what the different professions or disciplines had to offer. They also recorded tensions, however, in particular between those YOT staff who came from a youth justice social work background and those who were not familiar with or experienced in social work values and practices. These tensions in part centred on the shift in emphasis within the youth justice system as a whole from a 'welfare' orientation, which emphasised the value of direct work with young people, to a 'managerialist' approach, which prioritised information analysis as the basis for decision making, standardised assessment procedures and monitoring and recording systems (Burnett and Appleton, 2004, p 40). While 'mainstream' social work has itself changed substantially in recent years as a result of managerialist influences, there is clearly a challenge for social workers moving into a new operational environment where they have not only to adjust to such system pressures but also to colleagues with different values and assumptions about ways of working. In the YOT studied by Burnett and Appleton, the outcome was an overall tendency toward the 'fruit cake' model of the generic YOT worker, in which individual staff gradually lost their sense of identity with their original agency and professional backgrounds, but in which the distinctive values and skills associated with the 'direct work' approach of social work came to influence the non-social work staff and thus gave the 'cake' a specific kind of texture (Burnett and Appleton, 2004, p 41).

Similar findings were reported in a study of seven Welsh YOTs (Field, 2007). Here, too, there had been a gradual process of mutual understanding and learning across professional boundaries, with various tensions and disagreements. But an important trend was a continuing emphasis on the significance of social work goals concerned with young people's welfare as a core element of the response to youth offending, and a growing acceptance of this by other, non–social work, partners.

The multidisciplinary nature of YOTs is viewed as an important advantage in responding to the diversity of young people's circumstances, and the approach is carried forward into a number of programmes and services delivered at the local level. Some of these are discussed in the following section.

Partnership working for effective practice

In attempting to prevent offending and reoffending by children and young people, the YJB is 'committed to identifying and promoting effective practice … based on best practice and research evidence' (YJB, 2003a, p 1). Consequently, the YJB has published 15 'manuals' describing the features of effective services, based on systematic reviews of the research literature, and identifying staff and organisational learning and development needs. These 'manuals' are known as 'Key Elements of Effective Practice' (KEEPs).

The KEEPs are linked to the Effective Practice Quality Assurance (EPQA) cycle and associated Framework (YJB, 2006), designed to allow practitioners and managers, and therefore the YJB, to monitor performance against each of the identified KEEPs. The Framework is organised around eight 'core areas' seen to be common to all aspects of the youth justice system, namely:

- assessment
- individual needs
- communication
- service delivery
- training
- management
- service development
- monitoring and evaluation.

The following discussion explores these eight 'core areas', drawing on a number of the KEEPs documents in order to consider the important role played by partnership working in delivering effective, evidence-based practice within the youth justice system. A number of these 'core areas' include aspects of practice that rely on interprofessional and inter-agency partnership working, both within the YOT and externally. In particular, assessment, service development, service delivery and individual needs are most effectively addressed through partnership working. Other 'core areas', such as training, communication and management, will be seen to represent key factors in the facilitation of such partnership working.

Partnership working in service delivery

The effective assessment of young people is seen to necessitate information being 'gathered from a range of different sources and verified where possible' (YJB, 2003a, p 5). As such, assessment requires interaction with a broad group of practitioners and agencies. Typically this might include liaison with schools, social services and YOT staff who have previously worked with the young person. In addition, specialist knowledge may be required in relation to certain aspects of the assessment. For example, effective mental health assessment may require the involvement of health staff from custodial institutions, Child and Adolescent Mental Health Services (CAMHS) and a general practitioner (GP).

The collation of such information does, however, require consideration of the varying approaches and conceptual frameworks by which different professions interpret and explore circumstance and behaviour. To continue the example of mental health assessment, it is possible that in relation to the same child, 'A YOT team member may talk about a young person engaging in antisocial activity, a teacher about poor concentration and aggressive behaviour, and a social worker or youth worker may perceive a needy, anxious, abused child' (Walker, 2003, cited in YJB, 2003d, p 106).

The assessment undertaken by the YOT officer is designed to highlight individual needs across a broad range of issues. The primary assessment tool used within the YOT is the ASSET, completed for every young person who comes in contact with the youth justice system (Baker et al, 2003). The ASSET-based assessment process reflects the multitude of risk and protective factors identified by research to be associated with youth crime (YJB, 2001), including an offending history, attitudes towards offending, living arrangements, education, training and employment, drug or alcohol abuse, physical, emotional and mental health, as well as their general lifestyle circumstances.

As such, an ASSET assessment seeks to highlight the variety of factors impacting upon the individual's risk of offending that need to be addressed. This implies that 'A wide range of interventions should be available to reflect the complexity of risks and needs presented by young people' (YJB, 2003a, p 5). That is, the services available to a YOT need to reflect the full range of provision necessary to address the risk factors presented by young people, as well as the different degrees or levels of intensity of provision required.

The risk and resilience framework on which the ASSET assessment is based recognises that risk and protective factors act in combination. This implies a necessity for services to work in parallel to address such needs holistically.

> A system of care made up of multiple agencies working together acknowledges that troubled children have multiple needs that require, at different times, different combinations of a broad range of health and social care agencies. (Walker, 2003, cited in YJB, 2003d, p 105)

Similarly, McGuire's (1995) review of 'what works' in preventing reoffending identified multi-modal programmes as the most consistently effective in addressing the multiple and diverse needs of young people. The delivery of such programmes necessitates access to a broad range of diverse provision.

Professionals within the youth justice system face challenges in providing such holistic support (NAO, 2004). One of the main difficulties facing youth justice practitioners and managers is that they are not the primary providers of many of the required services. For example, in relation to education, employment and training opportunities, effective links are required with the local education authority (including education welfare services); individual schools and colleges; Connexions; Learning and Skills Councils; youth services; and library services. Similarly, external providers are required in order to address aspects of support relating to accommodation issues; benefits advice; family mediation; employment advice; leisure activities; money advice; and budget management. As such, youth justice workers are dependent on a range of other providers and partner agencies in order to successfully achieve desired outcomes, while attempting to provide a programme of support to young people that is experienced as integrated and coherent. A prominent example of such provision is the Intensive Supervision and Surveillance Programme (see Practice Example 1).

Practice Example 1

Intensive Supervision and Surveillance Programmes (ISSPs)

ISSPs are targeted at persistent young offenders and those who have committed more serious offences. It is a highly intensive approach, combining supervision and surveillance. Schemes comprise a range of components, including assessment; close monitoring; regular contact; and tagging; and modules such as education and training; changing offending behaviour; restorative justice; interpersonal skills; and family support. Additional modules can address an individual young offender's specific needs, such as mental health or drug and alcohol issues. Schemes are delivered by specialist ISSP teams.

Research (Moore et al, 2004) found a variety of organisational arrangements for local ISSPs, some linked to a single YOT while others served a consortium of YOTs; most ISSP teams operated within existing YOT structures, although a small number were managed by non-YOT agencies. Constructive relations were found between ISSP and YOT staff in just over half of the schemes studied, while in others there were tensions arising from confusions over roles and responsibilities, or differences of view about the value of certain ISSP components, such as electronic tagging – although the research found that such tensions reduced over time. With regard to external relations, ISSP workers in some schemes had difficulties in accessing education, accommodation, and mental health and drugs services; although the researchers report that successful multi-agency schemes were delivered in most instances. The effectiveness of such partnership working is seen to be dependent on a coordinated and planned approach to a particular case, involving a shared understanding of the roles to be played by each agency, and regular feedback on progress to each partner agency.

Thus, in order to deliver an initiative such as an ISSP, the responsible agency requires links with a number of departments and organisations, in order to provide all necessary components of provision and to ensure the necessary 25-hour contact time required with the young offender. Moore et al (2004) provide examples of the diverse agencies involved, including Connexions, health services and social services. As well as engaging programme providers, ISSP staff are also commonly engaged with mainstream agencies, such as schools, to encourage them to work with previously excluded young people; for example, the national evaluation of ISSPs found that only 19% of young people subject to the scheme were in mainstream education (Moore et al, 2004).

Such partnership working is also enshrined in legislation governing the roles and responsibilities of YOTs and their partner agencies. For example, Multi-agency Public Protection Arrangements (MAPPAs) were introduced by the 2000 Criminal Justice and Court Services Act and the 2003 Criminal Justice Act to address the need to protect the public when resettling 'dangerous offenders'. This legislation places a responsibility on the police, the National Probation Service, the Prison Service and YOTs (among other agencies) to identify young people who are eligible for referral; to share relevant information across agencies involved in risk assessment; to assess the risk; and to manage that risk.

Effective monitoring and evaluation of provision also requires collaboration. Data necessary to evaluate outcomes may be collected by other agencies. For example, access to information regarding educational attendance and attainment requires agreements with the local education authority. Equally, programmes of provision delivered by multiple agencies require combined evaluation allowing for intricate analysis of attribution and combined effect.

Facilitating partnership working

The above discussion suggests a number of prerequisite 'building blocks' for effective practitioner partnership working. Adopting the terminology of the YJB 'Key Elements of Effective Practice', these can be loosely grouped under the headings 'communication', 'management' and 'training'.

Communication

Communication clearly represents a key aspect of partnership working, making it a requirement for effective practice in relation to a number of the other core areas of practice identified within each KEEP.

Communication is of particular importance to programmes that rely on partnership in delivery. Two differing examples include Youth Offender Panels (see Practice Example 2) and ISSPs. The YJB emphasises the importance of communication to the effectiveness of Youth Offender Panels, suggesting that the disparate Panel membership 'should be given a clear explanation of what will happen and appropriate support and information to enable them to participate in it' (YJB, 2003f, p 5). ISSP is seen to require 'good two-way communication to ensure that these agencies understand the aims of the programme, the precise service that is required and the obligations on them, for example in terms of reporting non-attendance' (YJB, 2003b, p 9).

Practice Example 2

Youth Offender Panels

The 1999 Youth Justice and Criminal Evidence Act introduced the Referral Order as the primary sentencing disposal for all 10- to 17-year-old offenders who plead guilty and are convicted for the first time. The Order means that the young offender is referred to a Youth Offender Panel, whose responsibility it is to agree a 'contract' with the young offender that sets out a programme of activity that will help prevent further offending. The Panels are guided by principles of restorative justice, so there is an assumption that activities undertaken by the young offender will include some form of reparation towards the victim or the wider community. The Panels are organised and supported by the YOT, and comprise at least two members of the local community together with a YOT representative. Other people attending the Panel meeting, in addition to the young person and (if under 16 years) one or both parents, can include the victim or a representative of the wider community, a victim supporter, a supporter of the young person and anyone else whom the Panel believe can exert a positive influence on the young person.

Youth Offender Panels offer a different perspective on partnership working for youth justice staff. Here, the partnership is not so much with other agencies (although there are important issues about relationships with the police and the courts) but with lay people: the community members of the Panel, the victim, the parents of the young offender and possibly other participants in the Panel process. It is appropriate to consider this as a form of 'partnership' because, as the main research evaluation of Youth Offender Panels points out (Crawford and Newburn, 2003), all these people are made actively responsible for the outcomes of the process, along with the YOT staff. Among many other issues, the research raises the following key sources of difficulty in the YOT worker/lay person partnership:

- The relationship of the YOT Panel member to the community Panel members is confused by the dual nature of the YOT member's role, as both an advisor to the Panel and a decision maker – the accountability of the YOT member for Panel decisions becomes uncertain in situations where their advice has not been followed.

- There are issues regarding the follow-up to and review of the contract agreement and the young person's compliance – because of demands on their time, it can be difficult to get the same community members involved in review meetings, which is frustrating for YOT staff (and potentially unfair to the young person).
- There can be difficulties with victim involvement because of the need to encompass the emotional and expressive needs of victims that do not sit easily with administrative pressures to get Panels organised and decisions made rationally and efficiently.
- The relationship with the young person's parents may be made difficult by the problem of holding parents to account when they have agreed to contribute to the young person's engagement in restorative activities but then fail to do so.

Management

Effective partnership working is also necessarily reliant on strategic or system-level structures and agreements. While this is primarily the responsibility of YOT management, there are a number of implications for youth justice practitioners.

As noted above, the provision of programmes of support to young people requires links with a number of external, specialist providers. As such, systems for referral are required with education providers, local employers, mental health services, leisure facilities and so on. Issues of assessment, monitoring and evaluation suggest the need for systems to govern the flow of information between the range of agencies and professionals within the youth justice system. For example, the KEEP for remand management suggests that 'There should be systems in place to collect, record, verify and provide information to parents/carers, the Crown Prosecution Service, defence solicitors, pre-sentence report authors, accommodation providers and secure establishments' (YJB, 2003e, p 5).

Such agreement is typically secured through negotiation within strategic partnerships. The YOT has its own steering group, which includes representation from a range of relevant agencies and service providers. There are also a number of specialist forums associated with local youth courts, such as youth court user groups and youth court liaison meetings. These forums involve practitioners as well as managers, and 'help build working relationships, provide feedback on service delivery and develop local ... services' (YJB, 2003e, p 12).

Through such liaison, YOT strategies should be made 'compatible with other strategic plans' (YJB, 2003e, p 5). This might involve shared targets such that the aims and objectives of the YOT regarding youth crime prevention are understood and agreed by all agencies and professionals. For example, 'The YOT should participate in and support the development of cross-agency agreements with regard to the swift administration of justice' (YJB, 2003g, p 5). The development of such shared understandings has particular applications for partnership working with other social work and social care agencies. For example, care leavers are particularly at risk of developing problems of drug misuse (Ward et al, 2003), suggesting a need for coordinated action between youth justice provision and social services Leaving Care Teams.

Training

The above discussion also highlights a number of aspects of the training of youth justice practitioners that are necessary for the effective functioning of partnership delivery. Professionals throughout the system need to know when a referral should be made to a specialist agency. The example above in relation to mental health illustrated the need 'to equip practitioners with the skills and knowledge required to identify when to consult with and make referrals to mental health staff working with their local services' (YJB, 2003c, p 5). Such referral is clearly also dependent on a knowledge of who to refer to. Practitioners should know how to access information about the range, quality and appropriateness of the services available locally.

This also suggests the need for a broad, if relatively basic, knowledge of key issues upon which a referral might be dependent. For example, an awareness of indicators of substance misuse should be incorporated into the training and development of all those involved in the youth justice system (YJB, 2003f, p 5). In relation to mental health, training 'should cover the developmental nature of adolescence, the range of mental health issues facing children and young people within the youth justice system and the effective interventions available' (YJB, 2003c, p 15). In relation to both substance misuse and mental health provision, early intervention is key, yet specialist provision limited. The role played by other professionals is therefore vital. As such, YOT workers need to be 'alert and responsive' to changing needs, especially during high-risk times such as periods on remand or pre-trial (YJB, 2003d). However, the development of the generic skills implied by the requirement for such a broad, yet basic, knowledge further reinforces the concern regarding the potential 'deskilling' of specialist staff within the youth justice setting (Burnett and Appleton, 2004, p 41).

Conclusion

The current system of youth justice in England and Wales is both grounded in a partnership form of organisation, the YOT, which provides the primary means of coordinating responses to individual young offenders, and reliant on networks of multi-agency relationships to ensure delivery of required services. This poses challenges for social workers in the youth justice system. The first is to ensure that the core values and principles of social work, based on understanding and responding to the full range of the individual's personal and social needs, are not marginalised by the narrow focus on the prevention of offending which provides the 'common purpose' of the various partner agencies. The second challenge is to sustain a model of reflective and effective social work practice, which, in recognising that common purpose, seeks to balance accountability to other partners and to the system as a whole with the exercise of professional discretion and judgement in working with young offenders in ways that maximise the potential for beneficial outcomes (Eadie and Canton, 2002).

A particular, potentially uncomfortable, balance is required between the need to support the individual young person and the need to protect the wider public good. This brings ethical and value-based dilemmas and requires the practitioner to develop clarity around roles, responsibilities and value frameworks (Dugmore and Pickford, 2006).

At the same time, the new arrangements present clear opportunities. There is some research evidence that social workers within YOTs are able to influence the practice of other professionals by demonstrating the worth of social work methods of engaging with young people (Burnett and Appleton, 2004; Field, 2007); there is potential to assert effective methods of social work intervention in partnership settings. Beyond this, the multi-agency context provides the opportunity for youth justice social workers to form alliances with other professionals whose view of young people is not shaped solely by their offending behaviour. Social workers should seek out common ground with workers in services such as education, health, youth work and community development, and build on this to develop models of effective and holistic inter-agency practice with young offenders. And certain developments, such as the Young Offender Panels and other restorative justice initiatives premised on the active participation of the young offender, offer settings in which social work skills can be used to establish productive alliances with service users and other citizens.

The above discussion has illustrated that youth justice systems, and in particular YOTs, operate at the interface between professional frameworks, identities, roles and responsibilities. However, we have also demonstrated the specific knowledge, skill and value base belonging to youth justice practice, not least in the complex demands of balancing aspects of care and control.

As such, youth justice represents a key area in which professional social work and social care skills are necessary and valuable, yet one in which these skills may be challenged, countered and contradicted.

Trigger questions

- ➲ What are the key tensions for social work within a youth justice setting?

- ➲ What specific skills can social work bring to youth justice services?

- ➲ Can the anti-oppressive values framework of social work usefully influence youth justice practitioners?

Recommended resources

- ➲ The YJB provides updates on government policy and practice guidance and relevant literature. See www.yjb.gov.uk

- ➲ The National Association for Youth Justice promotes the rights of, and justice for, children in trouble. It offers relevant literature, practice information and regular newsletters. See www.nayj.org.uk

- ➲ The National Youth Agency was founded in 1991. It aims to advance youth work to promote young people's personal and social development, and their voice, influence and place in society. It is funded primarily by the Local Government Association and government departments. See www.nya.org.uk

References

Bailey, R. and Williams, B. (2000) *Inter-agency Partnerships in Youth Justice*, Sheffield: University of Sheffield Joint Unit for Social Service Research.

Baker, K., Jones, S., Roberts, C. and Merrington, S. (2003) *The Evaluation of the Validity and Reliability of the Youth Justice Board's Assessment for Young Offenders: Findings from the First Two Years of the Use of ASSET*, London: Youth Justice Board.

Bandalli, S. (2000) 'Children, responsibility and the new youth justice', in B. Goldson (ed) *The New Youth Justice*, Lyme Regis: Russell House.

Bateman, T. (2006) 'Youth crime and justice: statistical "evidence", recent trends and responses', in B. Goldson and J. Muncie (eds) *Youth Crime and Justice*, London: Sage Publications.

Burnett, R. and Appleton, C. (2004) 'Joined-up services to tackle youth crime: a case study in England', *British Journal of Criminology*, vol 44, no 1, pp 34–54.

Crawford, A. and Newburn, T. (2003) *Youth Offending and Restorative Justice*, Cullompton: Willan.

DfES (Department for Education and Skills) (2003) *Every Child Matters: Green Paper*, Cm 5860, Norwich: The Stationery Office.

DfES (2004) *Every Child Matters: Change for Children in Social Care*, Nottingham: DfES.

DfES (2005) *Youth Matters*, London: The Stationery Office.

Drakeford, M. and McCarthy, K. (2000) 'Parents, responsibility and the new youth justice', in B. Goldson (ed) *The New Youth Justice*, Lyme Regis: Russell House.

Dugmore, P. and Pickford, J. (with Angus, S.) (2006) *Youth Justice and Social Work (Transforming Social Work Practice)*, Exeter: Learning Matters.

Eadie, T. and Canton, R. (2002) 'Practising in a context of ambivalence: the challenge for youth justice workers', *Youth Justice*, vol 2, no 1, pp 14–26.

Field, S. (2007) 'Practice cultures and the "new" youth justice in (England and) Wales', *British Journal of Criminology*, vol 47, no 2, pp 311–30.

Holdaway, S., Davidson, N., Dignan, J. et al (2001) *New Strategies to Address Youth Offending: The National Evaluation of the Pilot Youth Offending Teams*, London: Home Office.

Home Office (1997) *No More Excuses: A New Approach to Tackling Youth Crime in England and Wales*, Cm 3809, London: HMSO.

Home Office (2003) *Youth Justice: The Next Steps*, London: Home Office.

McGuire, J. (ed) (1995) *What Works: Reducing Re-offending – Guidelines from Research and Practice*, New York: John Wiley & Sons.

Moore, R., Gray, E., Roberts, C., Merrington, S., Waters, I., Fernandez, R., Hayward, G. and Rogers, R.D. (2004) *ISSP: The Initial Report on the Intensive Supervision and Surveillance Programme*, London: Youth Justice Board.

Muncie, J. (1999) *Youth and Crime: A Critical Introduction*, London: Sage Publications.

Nacro (2006) *Some Facts about Children and Young People who Offend – 2004*, Youth Crime Briefing: March 2006, London: Nacro.

NAO (National Audit Office) (2004) *Youth Offending: The Delivery of Community and Custodial Sentences*, London: NAO.

Newburn, T. (2002) 'Young people, crime and youth justice', in M. Maguire, R. Morgan and R. Reiner (eds) *The Oxford Handbook of Criminology*, Oxford: Oxford University Press.

Pitts, J. (2001) *The New Politics of Youth Crime: Discipline or Solidarity?*, Basingstoke: Palgrave.

Prior, D. (2005) 'Evaluating the new youth justice: what can practitioners learn from research?', *Practice*, vol 17, no 2, pp 103-12.

Respect Task Force (2006) *Respect Action Plan*, London: The Stationery Office.

Smith, R. (2003) *Youth Justice: Ideas, Policy, Practice*, Cullompton: Willan.

Squires, P. and Stephen, D.E. (2005) *Rougher Justice: Anti-social Behaviour and Young People*, Cullompton: Willan.

Walker, S. (2003) 'Multidisciplinary family support in child and adolescent mental health services', *Journal of Clinical Child Psychology and Psychiatry*, vol 8, no 2, pp 215-26.

Ward, J., Henderson, Z. and Pearson, G. (2003) *One Problem among Many: Drug Use among Care Leavers in Transition to Independent Living*, Home Office Research Study No. 260, London: Home Office.

YJB (Youth Justice Board) (2001) *Risk and Protective Factors Associated with Youth Crime and Effective Interventions to Prevent It*, London: YJB.

YJB (2003a) *Key Elements of Effective Practice, Assessment, Planning Interventions and Supervision*, Edition 1, London: YJB.

YJB (2003b) *Key Elements of Effective Practice, Intensive Supervision and Surveillance Programmes*, Edition 1, London: YJB.

YJB (2003c) *Key Elements of Effective Practice, Mental Health*, Edition 1, London: YJB.

YJB (2003d) *Effective Practice Reader: Mental Health*, London: YJB.

YJB (2003e) *Key Elements of Effective Practice, Remand Management*, Edition 1, London: YJB.

YJB (2003f) *Key Elements of Effective Practice, Substance Misuse*, Edition 1, London: YJB.

YJB (2003g) *Key Elements of Effective Practice, Swift Administration of Justice*, Edition 1, London: YJB.

YJB (2006) *Key Elements of Effective Practice: Quality Assurance Framework: Guidance for Youth Offending Teams and Secure Establishments*, London: YJB.

Bringing together child health and social care provision: challenges and opportunities for multi-agency working[1]

Jane Coad

Introduction

This chapter will explore current health and social care provision and assumptions in relation to children's services. (Unless specifically stated, the term 'children' is used throughout the chapter to refer to both children and young people under the age of 18.) It will draw on empirical evidence and case studies to show how children's health and social care services are changing. One aspect of that change is the need for multi-agency working and multi-agency partnerships across health and social care. This partnership between the National Health Service (NHS) and social services has attracted much attention, and this chapter will explore this relationship.

The chapter begins with a brief review of the development of children's services within the field of health and social care. It will critically examine the different theoretical assumptions that underlie and shape the way in which children are viewed, and in turn how this impacts on multi-agency working, including social work activity. Two key themes will frame the discussion: first, the impact on the professionals of joint working, and second, the impact of multi-agency working on the children and families who use health and social care services. The discussion will be underpinned by examples from joint multi-agency work drawn from a wide range of health and social care settings and contexts. The challenges and opportunities when working across multi-agency teams will also be outlined in order to explore common messages for improving the delivery of health and social care services.

BOX 3.1: *Glossary of terms used*	
CAF	Common Assessment Framework
CAMHS	Child and Adolescent Mental Health Services
CDC	Child Development Centre
CT	children's trust
CYPP	Children and Young People's Plan
GP	general practitioner
JAR	Joint Area Review
LDP	Local Delivery Plan
NHS	National Health Service
NSF	National Service Framework
PCT	primary care trust
SHA	strategic health authority

Background: children's health services – how do they all fit together?

In order to answer this question we need to first consider the aim of the NHS in the UK: it is to improve the health and wellbeing of the population by promoting better health, to help prevent illness and to provide the best treatment and care when needed. Within the NHS, since 2004, the mechanism for improving the health of children and young people is the National Service Framework (NSF) for Children, Young People and Maternity Services, which is a 10-year programme launched by the Department of Health, designed to bring about sustained improvement in children's health and wellbeing.

The Department of Health sets national standards designed to improve service quality, secures resources and makes investment decisions to ensure that the NHS is able to deliver services. The Department of Health works with key partners, such as the Department for Education and Skills and the NHS Modernisation Agency, to ensure the quality of services. At a local level the responsibility for the organisation of services falls to different authorities and trusts. As there are a multitude of associated key terms, some of these are outlined in Box 3.2.

BOX 3.2: *Key partners in health and social organisations*

Strategic health authorities
Until 2006, there were 28 strategic health authorities (SHAs), created by the government in 2002 to manage the local NHS. Following reconfiguration this evolved into 10, with a much wider role of integrating health and social care services but remaining the key link between the Department of Health and local NHS trusts.

SHAs are responsible for developing plans for:

- improving health services in their area;
- making sure that services are of a high quality and performing well;
- increasing the capacity of local services;
- making sure that national priorities are integrated into local health service plans.

Within each SHA, services are split into various types of trusts that take responsibility for running the NHS at a more local level.

Primary care trusts
Primary care trusts (PCTs) manage all primary care services (such as general practitioners [GPs], pharmacists and dentists) but are also responsible for commissioning (or buying) almost all of the healthcare, both primary and secondary (known also as acute care), for the local population.

PCTs receive 75% of the NHS budget. As local organisations, they are thought to be in the best position to understand the needs of the local community and make sure that organisations providing health and social care are working effectively.

PCTs work with local authorities and other agencies that provide health and social care locally to make sure that the local community's needs are being met. They are responsible for getting health and social care systems working together to the benefit of patients.

Children's trusts
The government expects that all areas will have a children's trust (CT) arrangement by 2008. By 2006, each area had to have in place a Children and Young People's Plan (CYPP), which gave strategic direction for all children's services in a local area, and was designed in partnership with health, social care and other local partners such as education. Children's trusts build upon,

bring together and formalise this joint work and in that way work with the PCT. So, it is crucial that PCTs are involved when drawing up arrangements for cooperation for all children's services in the local area. Children's trusts will ensure that the NHS (PCT) and local authorities work closely together because it is felt that this is the best way to improve local health and social care services and outcomes for children and families.

Children's trusts are not legal entities but have been created to address the fragmentation of responsibilities for children's services. However, what gets commissioned in terms of local health and social care services will depend on 'local' need, for example community paediatrics, teenage pregnancy coordinators, health visitors, schools nurses, therapists, Child and Adolescent Mental Health Services (CAMHS), maternity services and/or palliative care.

Acute trusts
Hospitals are managed by acute trusts, which make sure that they provide high-quality healthcare and spend their money efficiently. They also decide on the strategy for how the hospital will develop, so that services improve.

Some acute trusts are regional or national centres for more specialised care; others are attached to universities and help to train health professionals. Acute trusts may sometimes provide services in the community (for example through clinics or health centres).

The extent of the involvement acute trusts will have in the development of children's trusts will vary between localities. This is because a number of acute trusts are still responsible for the delivery of some community-based services to children and because there is flexibility locally about which services should be included in children's trusts. So some children's trusts may commission services from acute trusts and some not. Whatever model is agreed, it will be essential for the children's trusts to have strong links to local acute trusts and to ensure that effective protocols are in place to ensure that child- and family-focused, integrated working occurs.

Foundation trusts (known as PFI trusts)
These are the newest type of NHS acute hospital trusts. They have been given more financial and operational freedom than other NHS trusts and have come to represent the government's commitment to decentralising control of public services. Foundation trusts remain within the NHS and its performance inspection system.

Special health authorities
These are health authorities that provide a national (rather than local) service, either to the public or to the NHS, for example NHS Direct, the National Blood Authority and the Health Development Agency. They are independent, but can be subject to ministerial direction like other NHS bodies.

Within the NHS, at a local level, there is a basic five-stage delivery cycle for the provision of services to children and young people. These stages can be seen as a continuous cycle of improvement, which mirror those that children's trusts will follow in planning and joint commissioning services. The five stages include, first, *assessing* the needs of children, young people and pregnant women (gathering, analysing and interpreting information to plan and improve services systematically), which then helps to *identify priorities*. From the identified priorities, targets and standards are set. These must be *planned and delivered jointly* with local partners, which include local authorities, and according to the PCT's three-year Local Delivery Plan (LDP) and the CYPP. Any subsequent *improvements* in the joint commissioning of services to meet specific needs of children, young people and families (based on the LDP and CYPP) are then *monitored and assessed* by a variety of internal evaluations, performance management, inspection by the Healthcare Commission and other inspectorates, and most recently Joint Area Reviews (JARs). JARs will be conducted by Ofsted in partnership with the Healthcare Commission and other inspectorates to look at how local services are cooperating. The new inspection framework will look at how health bodies are contributing to improved health and social care outcomes for children and young people.

The drivers to the current changes

Having provided an overview of the arrangements in place in health and social care services, consideration will now be given to some of the key drivers that have had a significant impact on the delivery of children's health services. The death of Victoria Climbié was one such driver. She was a privately cared-for eight-year-old girl who came into contact with a range of service providers with concerns for her welfare and health (Laming Report, 2003). Individually, and collectively, services were highlighted as having failed to recognise and prevent the child abuse that led to her death. The evidence from the resulting inquiry confirmed many of the messages from previous inquiries into similar child protection failings: the imperative to see and listen to children and respond to their needs, and to improve the quality of communication and joint working. Subsequently, this report increased the government's commitment to vulnerable children and raised the profile for a coordinated approach to child protection services.

The 2004 Children Act heralded the development of greater collaborative working and shared budgets. In September 2004, the Department of Health also launched the new NSF, setting national standards for children's health and social services (and the interface with education), from before birth through to adulthood (DH, 2004). The first five core standards of the framework apply to universal services for all children; standards 6 to 10 apply to particular groups of children and young people (children who are ill, children in hospital, disabled children and children with complex needs, children who have mental health problems, and medicines for children) and standard 11 covers maternity services. The NSF standards are to be delivered in partnership with local authorities, and are intrinsic to the delivery of the outcomes framework. However, not only does the NSF include standards upon which services will be delivered, but it also includes details about how joint children's services will be inspected (see the comment on JARs above).

Because full implementation is expected to take up to 10 years, the NSF forms part of the NHS 'developmental standards' that NHS organisations must work towards and which will be taken into account by the Healthcare Commission, which inspects healthcare provision in accordance with national standards and other service priorities, and reports directly to Parliament on the state of healthcare in England and Wales.

The children's NSF is directed at everyone involved in the delivery of services to children, young people or pregnant women. Therefore, the NSF is an integral part of the *Every Child Matters: Change for Children* programme (DfES, 2004). This links directly to another key document, *Our Health, Our Care, Our Community* (DH, 2006), which is a White Paper on all community services. While not necessarily representing children and young people, in every chapter children's services are mentioned.

The major challenges that arise from these directives and documents are linked in that all these developments require multi-agency teams of professionals to plan and deliver services in a different way. This requires working together on workforce development, ensuring that the right skills and training are in place and that there is a clear process for joint commissioning for services. The next part of this chapter will consider the impact of such change; first in terms of multi-agency working and second in terms of children, young people and families.

Impact of multi-agency working on staff and organisational delivery

All the drivers mentioned in this chapter are intended to lead to a cultural shift that will result in services that are designed and delivered around the needs of children and their families, rather than around the needs of organisations. As a result, there has been a movement suggesting that *joined-up* health and social care services for children, young people and their families will be the way forward. In this way, it is envisaged that overlap will be reduced and resources including expertise will be 'pooled' together, for example joint targets for childhood obesity, teenage pregnancy and reducing infant mortality. While Hughes (1996) noted that the concept of joined-up thinking was hastily thought up and needed more planning, there are a number of examples that can be drawn upon that are successful in terms of health and social care settings (Roaf and Lloyd, 1995; Coad and Needham, 2005).

Another impact of the drivers outlined is that all local partners will need to ensure that the planning and performance assessment of service delivery is *jointly* planned and delivered. Key to the success of all these plans is how effectively local partners such as health and social care can demonstrate that they work together for children and young people. Commonly, the plans of delivery are referred to as the 'Team Around the Child'. An example from the West Midlands is set out in Practice Example 1. Traditionally, each service was separately commissioned and delivered, but more recently there is emerging evidence that, locally, teams are planning and delivering well thought-out joined-up services (Leathard, 2005; Percy-Smith and Walsh, 2006; Walsall teaching PCT, 2007; Martin, 2007). The case study in Practice Example 1 demonstrates that joined-up services can be worthwhile for both staff and children and families.

Practice Example 1

Team Around the Child: case study from Walsall teaching PCT

Aim: Through Joint Commissioning, to improve quality outcomes for children with complex needs and their families.

Why: Children aged 0–5 were seen at the Child Development Centre (CDC) by a doctor and were then referred on to a series of different professionals, from a range of statutory and voluntary agencies. This was a long and tortuous journey, often daunting for families concerned.

What: Commissioners agreed on an improved service, which was more coherent with information shared to benefit all concerned, and put the child at the centre of the care.

Elements of the redesigned service:
- new pathway informed by what children and parents wanted;
- parents only having to tell the child's story once;
- direct participation and control for parents over decision making;
- key worker in place for each family;
- improved teamwork for staff;
- better understanding of each other's roles by all professionals;
- more effective communication throughout the child's journey.

Positive outcomes include:
- Waiting lists for assessment have been significantly reduced.
- All new referrals are presented to a panel within seven days so there is earlier access to support.
- The team has shared aims and values, which reflect a shared vision of a family-centred service.
- The removal of a formal assessment process has reduced the level of stress on the family.
- Services have joined together to agree clear policies for an integrated referral process, including a single point of entry and a multi-agency referral panel.
- A parent-focused group has been established to monitor parental views and impact on the service provision.

With kind permission, from Walsall teaching Primary Care Trust (2007)

Another key element in terms of the impact on multi-agency working is that service providers will be expected to demonstrate the active involvement of children and young people in decision-making processes on matters that affect them (DH, 2003, 2004; DfES, 2004). Whether in the long term this improves health and social care services and makes a difference to citizens remains to be seen. This also brings further new challenges and opportunities for the personnel who deliver the services and the 'service users' who receive them.

From the discussion thus far in this chapter, it is clear that there are many challenges and opportunities that could be explored in terms of multi-agency professional working. The chapter will now focus discussion in four main areas: planning cycles, ways of working, joint training, and monitoring and sustainability.

Planning cycles

Planning cycles are important to understanding the type of organisational culture within which the various professionals work. Clarity about the purposes, objectives and boundaries of decision making are necessary in any planning work, as exemplified in the case outlined in Practice Example 1. One notable challenge is that the concept of partnership implies that the power is shared. In reality, this may not be feasible. Even if the leadership relationship is carefully considered and agreed, making partnerships work across different cultures can be very challenging. For example, some professions traditionally have strong power bases, such as medicine. Thus, understanding each other's different theoretical models that underpin working practices is essential – and ultimately goes beyond viewing multi-agency working as simply a structural change in work organisation. In planning for multi-agency working, time is required to understand the variety of roles demanded and also a listening culture in which partners feel able to freely express their views without judgement (Roaf and Lloyd, 1995). Percy-Smith and Walsh (2006, p 46) support this process when they state that 'multi-agency partnerships need to be based on a shared sense of ownership, power, reciprocity and co-operation'.

Ways of working

As already outlined, there has been an influx of policies about collective ways of working, which are now embedded in children's services across health and social care. However, there is less empirical evidence about the impact on health and social care workers and the children, young people and families. At first glance it would seem as though the phrase *'joined-up working'* is therefore simply wishful rhetoric. But this might be a simplistic view of what is an immense cultural shift for health and social care service planning and delivery. In part this is to do with the traditional delivery of healthcare, which has been provided in different settings to that of social care. Consequently, developing new ways of working based on a needs-led model of care pathways is immensely challenging.

One example of new ways of working is outlined in Practice Example 2, where health and social care is delivered for children with disabilities through joint commissioning and management.

Practice Example 2

Integrated care in Shropshire County Council and PCT

Aim: Integrated health and social care team for children with disabilities through a children's joint commissioning unit (Shropshire County Council and PCT).

What: The team is led by a jointly funded and accountable service manager who line manages the social care team, the county council occupational therapists, health staff in special schools, and CDC and community medical staff.

Elements of the redesigned service:

- Direct line management of the social care team, the county council occupational therapists, health staff in special schools, CDC and community medical staff.
- From 2008 the team will also be relocated to a new building, which will also house a special school, a designated children's centre and the Child Adolescent Mental Health (CAMH) and Learning Disability (LD) team.

Positive outcomes include:

- Services have joined together to provide a more integrated service for children with disabilities and a multi-agency referral panel.
- This means for the multi-agency workers that there is greater sharing and 'pooling' of resources and inevitably greater awareness of the different roles.

With kind permission, from Shropshire County Council and PCT (2007)

Another example of new ways of working is in response to the Common Assessment Framework (CAF), which when used should highlight to teams what the child and family need in an integrated model of care. Some professionals have integrated the CAF-assessed needs of the child and family into Joint Working Plans or Integrated Care Pathways. These are jointly planned around the needs of the child and family as opposed to diverse, even overlapping, service-led models of care. They are useful in that they ensure that there is a clear multi-agency outline of anticipated care, placed in an appropriate timeframe, to help a client or patient with a specific condition or set of symptoms or needs to move progressively through their 'experience' to positive outcomes. Such planning and delivery is also important because it can help to reduce unnecessary variations in care and outcomes. This includes potential variations in how confidentiality is addressed, for example around competing priorities. This means that multi-agency care professionals, including health and social workers, will be able to develop improved understanding of different roles and thus foster creative partnerships in their delivery of services. Examples include children and young people with mental health problems, chronic illnesses and child protection cases. However, to have real impact, there needs to be a commitment to ensuring that such individual needs are clearly identified in a planned approach as opposed to a crisis, reactive approach.

Joint training

In a multi-agency approach where health and social care staff may have come from different backgrounds and where staff may not understand each other's role, there is a need to provide ongoing joint training so that each *'partner'* understands the frameworks within which they will work, and the terms and language used. This raises immense challenges for the deliverers of health and social care. Traditionally, health courses such as nursing, medicine and public health are taught separately from social care training. This can result in a demarcation (separation) of roles where traditional boundaries are closely guarded. Equally, there are professional role and accountability issues, when a person is not trained or *'fit for purpose'* for the role being undertaken. Recently there has been some evidence of shared health and social care training in aspects of learning disability, mental health and focused shared issues, for example transcultural communication (RCN, 2007). Furthermore, in terms of children's services, the General Social Care Council, the General Teaching Council for England and the Nursing and Midwifery Council have produced a joint statement that sets out the values and dispositions underpinning effective interprofessional work (NMC, 2007). In all these examples, it is clear that the focus is not about standardising different professional backgrounds, but rather understanding the culture and language used in order to promote common understanding and a sense of shared purpose.

Nonetheless, for any integrated approach to be sustained there has to be in place a continuity plan, including adequate resources and funding dedicated to joined-up training and support of the staff. A study by Percy-Smith and Walsh (2006) exploring improvements in multi-agency services in Northamptonshire concluded that training and skills development was a key requirement for both personnel and participating children and young people. Percy-Smith and Walsh (2006) also suggested that lead postholders were the key to facilitating the development of any multi-agency work if catalytic change was to occur at strategic and operational levels. Openness and transparency about all aspects of the work (both the specific case and more generally) is required – including opportunities for exchanging local and national initiatives. Increased exposure to other agencies, joint working and shared learning can assist in breaking down traditional ways of working within and between professional groups.

Monitoring and sustainability

When all local authorities produced a CYPP (see Box 3.2 under 'Children's trusts') it was intended that this would serve to benchmark the new integrated services and enable inspection of the meeting of these plans. JARs are being conducted by Ofsted in partnership with the Healthcare Commission and other inspectorates to look at how local services are collaborating. The obvious implication of this is that multi-agency professionals will be able to share data about children, young people and families with the aim of reducing overlap. But there is also a wider debate to consider in that sharing data may help to demystify professional language and culture, which can often act as a barrier when trying to understand different roles and professions.

The impact of multi-agency working on children and families

Giving meaningful choice to children, young people and their families represents a significant and recent change in policy and practice. At a national level, the Department of Health and Department for Education and Skills have encouraged the participation of children, young people and families in decision making (DfES, 2004; DH, 2004). Many authors, however, have noted that it must be appropriate, meaningful and not imposed (Coad and Lewis, 2004). This section of the chapter will focus discussion in the main areas of children and young people's participation. Examples from fieldwork and evidence will be drawn upon.

Participation

A key element to the success of joined-up services and working together is to understand how those who use the services respond to them. This raises the question of how effective children's participation can be within traditional systems, which are themselves not participatory but hierarchical. Thus, for children to become involved in influencing multi-agency services in terms of planning and delivery requires a culture shift in organisations seasoned with a liberal dose of critical reflexivity (Weil, 1998). Coad and Shaw (2006) and Coad and Houston (2007) in two comprehensive literature reviews found a plethora of information and policy documents about the need to facilitate participation of children, and young people, including some examples of good practice and useful toolkits to do this (Cohen and Emanuel, 1998; Fajerman et al, 2000; Fajerman, 2001; Wright and Haydon, 2002; Kirby et al, 2003).

One example where children have been involved in planning joined-up services is drawn from Coventry in the West Midlands (Coventry's Children and Young People's Strategic Partnership, 2007). Here, a number of key developments were planned to create a culture of involving children and young people. This included the setting up of The Coventry Partnership for Youth Board, which subsequently secured funding to create 'The Democracy Project', which aimed to develop structures, processes and motivational opportunities to engage young people in decision making. Young people were involved in the initial planning and empowered to take the lead and express their views. In this way, participation involves a culture of listening that enables children to influence decisions about the services they receive as individuals on a day-to-day basis, as well as how those services are developed and delivered to all children who access them (Wright et al, 2006). This in turn requires a shift in professional identities from experts to partners based on mutual respect and power sharing involving dialogue and collaboration between children and adults (Percy-Smith and Walsh, 2006).

However, there is limited evidence on the impact of children's involvement on organisational cultures. Coad and Houston (2007) found that most projects reviewed that discussed the involvement of users in the organisational culture were largely adult orientated (including agenda items, organisation of meetings, choice of methods, interpretation of results, service planning cycles). While children felt as service users that they did have a particular role to play in informing health and social care delivery, their impact on the organisation was variable. Willow (2002) also noted that some children felt devalued or not taken seriously by the professionals and while they had been asked to contribute to consultations their ultimate impact on changing the service was low.

Interestingly, some of the grey literature reviewed suggested that there was an argument for children not to attend adult service planning meetings and events (that is, that it would not be appropriate). Authors noted that adult-based events can be intimidating for children and that their views and choice should be incorporated through a system of a 'gatekeeper' (Coad and Lewis, 2004). Whatever mechanism is preferred, one of the implications of this for multi-agency working is that there needs to be a more active participation model as opposed to a passive consultation model.

A key dilemma is that participation initiatives are so often undertaken in contexts that are not participatory, which do not support organisational learning and change. Therefore, for children's participation to have a real impact, children need to be involved in whole systems learning and change (Percy-Smith and Walsh, 2006). Consequently, a framework of ongoing participatory monitoring of service initiatives and performance review in terms of children's participation should be developed if health and social care services are to progress forward. This would include tracking of the children and/or focused case examples, which will seek to evaluate the full impact of the multi-agency agenda from the perspectives of the users. This is particularly relevant to those who will have to act upon the findings and recommendations of the project, such as healthcare and social workers (Stafford et al, 2003).

The implication of participation for multi-agency service delivery is that children need to be put at the centre of the organisation's endeavours, rather than the service itself. This requires an accompanying shift in criteria for assessing outcomes from performance targets for service delivery to changes in children's wellbeing and circumstances.

Conclusion and future directions

In this chapter, it has been highlighted that health and social care provision has experienced rapid change both for those planning and delivering services and for the children, young people and families who receive them. Two key themes framed the discussion: first, the impact of joint working on the multi-agency professionals and, second, the impact on the children, young people and families involved.

While this chapter is not exhaustive, it does show that multi-agency professionals, including social workers, need not only to develop their skills in order to plan and deliver joined-up services but also to seriously consider the participation of the users, in this case children, young people and their families. Drawing on the evidence of this chapter, there are a number of factors that need to be in place for effective multi-agency working. One is that working arrangements need to be planned and agreed with a shared sense of ownership and cooperation. Multi-agency working across health and social care is not about homogenising different professional backgrounds but rather understanding the culture from where each comes in order to promote a common understanding and a sense of shared purpose.

Themes discussed in this chapter demonstrate that fundamental to the process is communication across agencies and between professionals, and a sense of trust so that openness and transparency of work is evident. In this way, multi-agency professionals can value and respect each other in terms of roles, expertise, skills and professional culture. This is essential if there are to be real benefits felt by children and families who receive the services delivered by multi-agency health and social care workers.

Trigger questions

➲ Can the key barriers to effective multi-agency working in child health and social care be identified?

➲ What might be some of the ways forward for the joint development of health and social care services for children?

➲ To what extent is it feasible or desirable for children to participate in multi-agency health and social care planning?

Recommended resources

➲ Aldgate, J., Healy, L., Malcolm, B., Pine, B., Rose, W. and Seden, J. (eds) (2007) *Enhancing Social Work Management Theory and Best Practice from the UK and USA*, London: Jessica Kingsley Publishers, pp 105-26.

➲ Coad, J. and Houston, R. (2007) *'Children's Voices': Involving Children and Young People in the Decision-making Processes of Health Care Service: A Review of the Literature*, London: Action for Sick Children.

➲ Fajerman, L. (2001) *Children are Service Users Too: A Guide for Consulting Children and Young People*, London: Save the Children.

➲ Fajerman, L., Jarrett, M. and Sutton, E. (2000) *Children as Partners in Planning: A Training Resource to Support Consultation with Children*, London: Save the Children.

Note

[1] Thanks to Sue Hatton, Workforce Development Specialist for Women and Children, NHS West Midlands; Sue Marsh, Policy Lead, Children's Services, Coventry PCT; Shropshire County Council; Donna Darbyshire, South Birmingham PCT; and Walsall teaching PCT for their kind permission to use materials.

References

Coad, J. and Houston, R. (2007) *'Children's Voices': Involving Children and Young People in the Decision-making Processes of Health Care Service: A Review of the Literature*, London: Action for Sick Children.

Coad, J. and Lewis, A. (2004) *Engaging Children and Young People in Research: Literature Review for the National Evaluation of the Children's Fund (NECF)*, 1 October, London: National Evaluation of the Children's Fund.

Coad, J. and Needham, J. (2005) *Snapshot: An Exploratory Survey of Young People's Perceptions of Health and Healthy Living using a Photographic Record*, Heart of Birmingham (HoB)tPCT Report, obtain from first author: Jane.coad@uwe.ac.uk

Coad, J. and Shaw, K. (2006) *'Children's Choice': A Systematic Literature Review of Children and Young People's Choice in Health Care Services and Information Choice*, Birmingham: Birmingham and Black Country PCT.

Cohen, J. and Emanuel, J. (1998) *Positive Participation: Consulting and Involving Young People in Health-related Work: A Planning and Training Resource*, London: Health Development Agency.

Coventry's Children and Young People's Strategic Partnership (2007) *Coventry PCT*, unpublished, for further details contact Sue Marsh, Coventry PCT.

DfES (Department for Education and Skills) (2004) *Every Child Matters*, Green Paper, London: DfES.

DH (Department of Health) (2003) *Children & Young People's Strategy*, London: DH.

DH (2004) *The National Service Framework for Children, Young People and Maternity Services*, London: DH.

DH (2006) *Our Health, Our Care, Our Community: Investing in the Future of Community Hospitals and Services*, London: DH.

Fajerman, L. (2001) *Children are Service Users Too: A Guide for Consulting Children and Young People*, London: Save the Children.

Fajerman, L., Jarrett, M. and Sutton, E. (2000) *Children as Partners in Planning: A Training Resource to Support Consultation with Children*, London: Save the Children.

Hughes, G. (1996) 'Strategies of multi-agency crime prevention and community safety in contemporary Britain', *Studies on Crime and Crime Prevention*, vol 5, no 2, pp 221-44.

Kirby, P., Lanyon, C., Cronin, K. and Sinclair, R. (2003) *Building a Culture of Participation: Involving Children and Young People in Policy, Service Planning, Delivery and Evaluation*, Research report DfES/0827/2003, Nottingham: DfES Publications.

Laming Report (2003) *The Victoria Climbié Inquiry*, Norwich: HMSO.

Leathard, A. (2005) 'Evaluating interagency working in health and social care: politics, policies and outcomes for service users', in D. Taylor and S. Balloch (eds) *The Politics of Evaluation*, Bristol: The Policy Press, pp 135-51.

Martin, V. (2007) 'Managing across interagency boundaries: a learning agenda for change', in J. Aldgate, L. Healy, B. Malcolm, B. Pine, W. Rose and J. Seden (eds) *Enhancing Social Work Management Theory and Best Practice from the UK and USA*, London: Jessica Kingsley Publishers, pp 105-26.

NMC (Nursing Midwifery Council) (2007) *Interprofessional Working*, www.nmc-uk.org.uk/interprof

Percy-Smith, B. and Walsh, D. (2006) *Improving Services for Children and Families: Listening and Learning*, Northampton: Children's Fund Northamptonshire/SOLAR.

RCN (Royal College of Nursing) (2007) *Resources, Transcultural Communication and Health Care Practice*, RCN online, www.rcn.org.uk/resources/transcultural/multiagency/index.php

Roaf, C. and Lloyd, C. (1995) 'Multi-agency work with young people in difficulty', *Findings: Social Care Research 68*, June, York: Joseph Rowntree Foundation.

Shropshire County Council and PCT (2007) *New Ways of Working*, unpublished PCT working document, for further details contact Shropshire County Council.

South Birmingham PCT (2007) *Looked after Nurse Service*, unpublished, for further details contact Donna Derbyshire, South Birmingham PCT.

Stafford, A., Laybourn, A., Hill, M. and Walker, M. (2003) 'Having a say: children and young people talk about consultation', *Children and Society*, no 14, pp 361-73.

Walsall teaching Primary Care Trust (2007) *Team Around the Child*, unpublished internal document, for further details contact Walsall tPCT.

Weil, S. (1998) 'Rhetorics and realities in public service organisations: systemic practice and organisational learning as critically reflexive action research', *Systemic Practice and Action Research*, vol 11, no 1, pp 37-62.

Willow, C. (2002) *Participation in Practice: Children and Young People as Partners in Change*, London: Children's Society.

Wright, P. and Haydon, D. (2002) *'Taking Part' Toolkit: Promoting the Real Participation of Children and Young People*, Manchester: North West Children's Taskforce.

Wright, P., Turner, C., Clay, D. and Mills, H. (2006) *The Participation of Children and Young People in Developing Social Care*, Participation Practice Guide 06, London: Social Care Institute for Excellence (SCIE), available from www.scie.org.uk/publicationspracticeguides, last accessed 3 January 2008.

Working with extended schools to prevent social exclusion

Anne Edwards, Apostol Apostolov, Irene Dooher and Anna Popova

It was 1.45, the pupils had been sent home so that staff could prepare for a parents' evening and I was sitting in the school's public foyer waiting for the rest of the research team to arrive. I opened the school's newsletter, full of its achievements, but was quickly distracted by the noise from one of the school's radio-controlled phones. The receptionist was talking with someone elsewhere on the campus, explaining that a year 10 pupil wanted to come into school to collect a piece of coursework she needed at home to continue to work on it. The next 10 minutes were taken up with noisy radio calls to the various entry points to the school to find out if the pupil could be permitted to re-enter the school and if so where. At one point she opened the door to the foyer to glimpse a part of the school she most certainly would not be allowed to enter as this was the part where it did its extended school work and was separated from the rest of the school by a card-swiped door in the linking corridor. The rest of the research team finally arrived, we moved on to our allocated room and the pupil remained in the outer foyer still trying to gain access to her work in her school. (Fieldnotes)

Schools are bounded systems

Seeing professional life from the perspective of potential partners is a first step in a move towards interprofessional collaboration and for that reason we are starting this chapter with a view of school life that would be shared by many teachers. Teaching is a risky business. It is often compared with being a circus ringmaster. Teachers in classrooms have to orchestrate a curriculum, the use of resources, and the individual learning trajectories of, often, as many as 35 learners at a time. All that happens within tightly timed lessons marked by the tyranny of the bell, which signals the moment of all change. At that point pupils leave for other lessons and teachers gather their belongings to move to different groups. So much depends on order in and out of classrooms. If order breaks down, everyone is hurt: teachers can't teach and pupils can't learn. But that order is often frighteningly fragile, and teachers in UK schools have, at least since the beginnings of state-funded education, worked hard to sustain it. Rule-bending, even letting a child into school when she should be at home, is not something that can be accommodated in some schools.

There have been several attempts over the years to downplay order and to be more child-centred; but it is not a strong theme in the recent history of state education in the UK (Edwards, 2001). Indeed, from the late 1970s until fairly recently, because of government directives, the main emphasis in schools has been on the curriculum and how it is delivered to children, including children who have special needs. This means that most teachers trained since the early 1980s have been obliged to focus on curricula and assessment first and the particular needs of individual children second. Of course there are many teachers and schools who have struggled against these emphases; but funding mechanisms and league tables of performance have made it difficult for them.

The focus on what has been called 'the standards agenda' rather than the children has had two effects. First, relations between home and school have come to be characterised by what one of us has described as the school's 'colonisation of the home' (Edwards and Warin, 1999, p 337), where, for example, parents of children who are not achieving in school are helped to support the school's curricular work. Rather than seeing the home as a source of what Moll and Greenberg have described as 'funds of knowledge' (Moll and Greenberg, 1990, p 320), which can be built on by teachers, these practices downplay home cultures. Second, troubled children tend to become visible when their troubles mean that they are not keeping up with the curriculum, through, for example, 'frequent absences', or when they prevent others from doing so by 'spoiling lessons'. (Both of these terms come from behaviour checklists in schools.) They are less likely to be visible if their troubles do not lead to disruption that might affect curriculum performance.

While in primary schools links between home and school are often informal as well as supported by systems of home–school liaison, in secondary schools the links are usually entirely formal. In addition, secondary schools have well-established systems of pastoral care, which start with the work of form tutors. Form tutors and class teachers are expected to pass problem pupils to the pastoral leads in each year group, who usually make up a pastoral team that is led by a member of the senior management team with responsibility for pastoral care. The team may be augmented by other teachers with, for example, particular responsibility for reintegrating children who have been excluded from school. In most schools the pastoral team is the point of contact for social workers. Schools have usually developed quite tight social practices through these teams, which are aimed at maintaining order and a focus on academic performance. These practices rarely relate to what else is going on in a child's life. Indeed a teacher with responsibility for pastoral care in his school once described the school as an island of safety in the following terms:

> 'If a child comes to school and they have come from a dreadful home situation where there is terrible violent crime and abuse and the parenting is poor or non-existent because of addiction problems and so on and so forth, the kid hasn't had much ... they can't read and write to any standard that enables them to learn and access the curriculum. And it is true to say that it can be awful out there, but you don't have to fail in school because we've got this for you, that person is there for you ... And I think it is a sanctuary.'

In all of what we have described so far, teachers are as much the victims of school practices as the pupils. Teacher retention is often seen as a problem in England and teachers cite workload and children's poor behaviour as reasons for leaving. So serious was the problem seen to be in 2003-04 that the House of Commons Select Committee for Education and Skills investigated recruitment and retention in order to advise the government. It is sometimes difficult to see schools from the perspectives of the teachers who struggle every day to sustain the order that is demanded of them and the professional identities that go with that, which often feel uncomfortable to them (Nias, 1990), but we think it is an important first step.

In this chapter we draw on work we have done in two research projects that have examined multi-agency working for children and families[1] and examine in particular interactions between education practitioners and children and families workers as they negotiate their practice. We have started by looking at schools as sets of tightly bounded systems because teachers are caught in those systems with very little freedom of movement, despite their apparent authority over pupils. We now move on to examine the implications of a recent attempt to rethink school boundaries.

BOX 4.1: *Glossary of terms used*	
DCSF	Department for Children, Schools and Families
DfES	Department for Education and Skills
ICT	information and communication technology
LMS	local management of schools
NECF	National Evaluation of the Children's Fund
OECD	Organisation for Economic Co-operation and Development
PAT	Policy Action Team

Extended schools

The Department for Education and Skills' (DfES) extended schools initiative (DEMOS, 2004; DfES, 2005) is now under the renamed Department for Children, Schools and Families (DCSF) currently trying to shift several decades of a heavy emphasis on curricula. It is potentially an opportunity for schools to join in work on preventing social exclusion by looking across a child's life and intervening with other services to prevent exclusion. By social inclusion we mean being able to access and contribute to the benefits that society offers its citizens. While this may be a somewhat normative definition, it reflects government intentions and is a much broader definition of inclusion than the one used in schools from the 1980s onwards. Then, inclusion meant helping children to access the school curriculum. Interprofessional collaboration, as we shall see, involves recognising that words may have different meanings for different professional groups. These differences can range from misunderstandings over whether a 'ward' refers to a neighbourhood or part of a hospital or whether 'assessment' is a detailed diagnostic overview of all aspects of a child's needs or a test in a classroom; to shorthand such as 'at risk', which for social workers is likely to mean at risk of abuse, but within preventative frameworks with other professionals may mean vulnerability to social exclusion.

The importance of education in combating social exclusion was clear in the understandings developed in the 1990s by the Organisation for Economic Co-operation and Development (OECD) (Evans, 1995; OECD, 1998). The OECD view of social exclusion was primarily economic and based on an anxiety that alienated youngsters were 'at risk' of being unable to both benefit from and ultimately contribute to society: a particularly strong concern given the ageing population in most of Europe. The Policy Action Team (PAT) 12 report (Home Office, 2000) reflected these concerns about young people and risk, by recognising that vulnerability to social exclusion was not simply a feature of the early years of life and that, as a result of changing life circumstances, a young person could also become vulnerable.

Consequently, it suggested that early intervention needed to be recast to include early intervention at early signs of vulnerability, whatever the child's age. Of course, signs of vulnerability may not trigger a reaction unless an accumulated picture is constructed as a result of practitioners looking at several aspects of a child's life. The PAT 12 report therefore called for more flexible and responsive working with young people to both identify and respond to vulnerability.

The reaction of the English school sector to efforts to integrate provision for children, young people and families to enable looking across the different domains of a child's life was disappointing. This was mainly due to government education policy that gave priority to standards over wellbeing. For example, schools were not to be included in most of the early children's trusts. These were the first attempts at integrating services for children and have informed the development of the new directorates that have brought together the management of services for children and families and education in local authorities.

Schools were able to remain isolated from the initiatives occurring in local authorities because of changes made by the Thatcher government's education policies in the 1980s. In order to reduce the powers of the local authorities over education so that government could fast-track its curriculum reforms, increasing powers were given to individual schools through initiatives such as the 'local management of schools' (LMS). LMS meant that instead of funding to schools being mediated by local authorities, the majority went directly to individual schools, with a limited amount being held by local authorities for pared-down central services. One result of many outcomes of LMS is that teachers are now employed by schools and not the local authority. Schools now have over 20 years' experience of being autonomous, self-running organisations, placed in a competitive marketplace for both pupils and staff. Collaboration is rarely part of their recent history.

The extended school initiative, which talks of what schools should offer their communities, can therefore be seen as a strategy for building schools into current work on social exclusion in ways that respect the adjustments they have made as a result of government-led education policies since the late 1970s. In brief, the initiative intends that by 2010 all children will have access to a variety of activities beyond the school day (DfES, 2005). There is no uniform model of an extended school; however, the roll-out of the scheme is supported by a 'National Remodelling Team', which helps schools to develop their 'core offer', which, in summary, is as follows:

- high-quality wraparound care both before and after school either on the school site or offered by local providers with transport to and from the school;

- a varied menu of activities, which may include homework clubs, study support, music, dance, drama, sports, volunteering and so on;
- parenting support to help parents at 'key transition points' and parenting programmes run with the help of other children's services and family learning opportunities;
- 'swift and easy referral' to a wide range of specialist support services such as speech therapy, family support services and sexual health services, some of which may be delivered on school sites;
- the provision of community access to sport and ICT (information and communication technology) facilities and adult learning opportunities.

This is quite a modest, if not conservative, list of offers. Many of these services are not new to schools. Schools have for a long time run extended school days and opened their doors to community classes: a baseline survey of provision (Clemens et al, 2005) found that 95% of secondary schools and 87% of primary schools offered after-school activities, while several funding initiatives have encouraged schools to boost their sport and ICT facilities by making some of them also available to adults in their community.

Parenting support and attempts at speeding referral processes could indicate that some schools may not, in the future, be entirely dominated by the curriculum and may look at relationships with families and agencies outside the school to work with a more rounded view of the child. However, it is possible that such changes could be very slow. Both parenting support and improving referrals may do little to shift relationships between schools and other services so that schools work in more collaborative ways with other professionals.

Parenting support gives schools an extended education role rather than a responsive and collaboratively preventative one. It can also sometimes suggest a deficit model of the home, where parents need to be educated rather than being seen as potential partners in the support of their children's development. This approach has also been seen as naively optimistic about the power of education over poverty. Moran and Ghate (2005), for example, have observed how poverty reduces the effects of parenting programmes and have argued for the need to tackle social conditions alongside providing education. Speedy referral also does little to shift how schools are positioned in relation to other agencies. Although improved referral is appreciated by parents and carers, the core offer suggests that referral is from the school and onwards to other services and that feedback from other agencies to the school, for example to ask it to play an important part in the long-term support of the wellbeing of children, is not a major aspect of the work of extended schools. In our work on both research projects, for example, we were aware of the tendency in some schools to pass the problems with children who they had defined as troublesome pupils to other agencies, so that the schools could sustain their work on curricula without the disruption caused by these pupils.

A focus on passing a child to a range of different agencies to sort out problems identified by the school is not the most child-centred approach, as one practitioner illustrated:

> 'I think there's the issue ... of seeing the child as a whole rounded being, that we don't [ie shouldn't] look at the bits and send bits off to be sorted out. And then you get the bits together and we put them back together and we get a perfect child. It doesn't work like that.'

The evaluators of the extended schools pathfinders initiative picked up a similar concern about schools' attempts at defining what needs to be done to solve problems they have identified, this time from a community perspective: 'It is particularly important that extended schools do not fall into the trap of imposing professional views of what is "needed" on the communities they serve' (Cummings et al, 2004, p 4).

The aims and social practices of schools are deeply entrenched for the understandable reasons we have just outlined. The boundaries remain strong and the need for internal order paramount. Furthermore, it seems that it will be easy for the extended schools initiative to do little to erode them. So what is to be done?

Social work and early intervention for prevention

Just as schools and teachers have sound reasons for sustaining their existing practices, so do children and families workers. If teaching is a profession where the risk of disorder and possibly violence is always close by, many children and families workers face these risks daily and often while working alone in the community. They cannot easily prioritise the prevention of social exclusion over child protection as to do so would lay them open to charges of irresponsibility and endangering children.

There is also the matter of professional identity: to participate fully in the practices of their profession within local authority settings they need to keep focused on heavy end work (Jack, 2006). The professional culture of what was social work is still preoccupied with child protection, and even targeted family support is often centred on families whose needs mean that child protection might be the next option. It seems that to pull your weight in children and families work, you need to be doing the hard stuff that is protection. This is not a surprising situation. Not only is protection work at the core of professional identity, prevention work calls for a different sort of long-term multi-agency collaboration without the framework of child protection procedures. To do prevention work, practitioners need to leave the safety of their supportive professional cultures and strong procedures to work over time with people who may not only not know them, but also not trust them.

In Box 4.2 we have listed some of the documentation that begins to spell out the kinds of collaborations that will arise once the extended schools initiative is fully in place. It seems that for both teachers and social workers, if multi-agency working to prevent social exclusion is to occur it needs to be enabled by some adjustments at the level of the organisation. That is, schools and children and families services need to help collaboration to happen without leaving teachers or children and families workers vulnerable and exposed outside the safety of their home organisations. In both projects we saw so many examples of the hero-practitioner who blazed new trails and created new interprofessional relationships without the support of their organisations. Their work was often risky simply because it was not framed by procedures. It relied heavily on personal energy and commitment, and even if nothing went wrong, burn-out was common. The rules and procedures in home organisations have needed to change, so that more responsive interprofessional work could occur. Reducing hierarchies and timescales within organisations so that a practitioner who notices vulnerability can initiate collaborative responses is just one example of the kinds of changes we have seen emerge to help multi-agency work.

BOX 4.2: *Some of the statutory guidance related to the extended schools initiativ e*

- ■ *Every Child Matters: Change for Children* (DfES, 2004), www. everychildmatters.gov.uk
- ■ 2004 Children Act, www.opsi.gov.uk/acts/acts2004/20040031.htm
- ■ *National Service Framework for Children, Young People and Maternity Services* (DH, 2004), www.dh.gov.uk
- ■ *Extended Schools: Access to Opportunities and Services for All: A Prospectus* (DfES, 2005), www.dcsf.gov.uk
- ■ The Local Safeguarding Childrens Board Regulations 2006, Statutory Instrument 2006 No 90.
- ■ *Working Together to Safeguard Children: A Guide to Inter-agency Working to Safeguard and Promote the Welfare of Children* (DfES, 2006a), www.everychildmatters.gov.uk
- ■ *Parenting Support: Guidance for Local Authorities in England* (DfES, 2006b), www.everychildmatters.gov.uk/resources-and-practice/IG00169/
- ■ *Reaching Out: An Action Plan on Social Exclusion* (Cabinet Office, 2006), www.cabinetoffice.gov.uk/social_exclusion_task_force/reaching_out/

The way forward

Implications for organisations

Seeing expertise as distributed across local areas

The organisational adjustments are likely to be greatest in the schools, if only because they are so tightly bounded and allow most teachers very little freedom of movement to work responsively and flexibly with other professionals. As we have seen, there is little evidence from the extended schools initiative that these practices are to be disturbed, unless schools choose to work very differently. Nonetheless, we have moments of optimism. We have seen exciting developments in a number of local authorities that are helping schools to see themselves as a part of a local system of what we have been calling *distributed expertise*.

By distributed expertise we mean that in most localities we can find different kinds of good specialist knowledge that can be brought to bear in parallel to disrupt a child's trajectory from social exclusion so that they travel towards inclusion and are able to access and contribute to what society offers. That distributed specialist knowledge may include, for example, a family worker who knows how to support a child's carer, a housing charity that can help when needed, a mentoring programme that can build a child's confidence and study support that can help a child catch up on missed school work. We think that the idea of distributed expertise is important because it stops any idea of an all-purpose generalist practitioner who operates with a relatively low skill base across a number of different areas of child welfare. We are concerned about the potential for deskilling that prevention work might offer, and argue that it should be avoided.

In one authority we have studied, this networked approach has involved building new schools that incorporate a range of services for children and families, mirroring Sure Start models of co-location. In several others we have seen the development of multiprofessional teams and in others we have watched extended schools being drawn into local systems of service provision where they are seen as just one service among many. In this chapter we are focusing on the latter as they are the least structured and probably the most difficult situations for other professionals. They therefore raise questions that resonate across the other, more managed, models of interprofessional work.

In these local systems of distributed expertise a school is simply one of several services that might identify a need and one of several that might respond to a need identified by another service. This is a very different model from the one in which a school labels a troublesome child and passes them on to other services for treatment; or where a social worker is incorporated into the school system. The working practices in these distributed systems are still developing, but the message is clear that operating in this flexible and collaborative way will not only benefit children; it can also help workers to feel more supported by other practitioners. One convinced professional explained her vision of a distributed system after hearing a teacher talking about how isolated people working with vulnerable children in schools actually felt:

> 'One of the reasons for having things like full service extended schools is the balance of the people you keep bringing into the school. If you keep doing that the school will burst. Or do you have a school working with and across the boundary ... I think we are struggling towards a model [of an extended school] which is successful in terms of meeting the children's needs, the family's needs and Education's needs and the professionals in education.'

This statement was followed by a comment from a children and families worker that 'It's a massive agenda and it's more than a school's thing'. She was right: local networks of distributed expertise do not arise spontaneously; they of course need to be planned and coordinated or managed. But if they are to enable people to do risky work together and perhaps outside the safety of their organisations, attention also needs to be given to building trust across professional boundaries.

Creating systems of networked expertise

In the National Evaluation of the Children's Fund (NECF) (Edwards et al, 2006) we found that programme workers put a lot of effort into sustaining local interprofessional meetings. We were able to look at how some of these developed into thriving networks in our more detailed case studies. These examples are not a blueprint, but there are, we think, some useful lessons to be learnt from them. The process has been described elsewhere as 'springboard and trails' (Edwards, in press). In brief, it involved regular meetings of practitioners from different services including the voluntary sector. These meetings were either in neutral spaces or moved between different settings to ensure they were not owned by one service. They also had to be timed to ensure that all practitioners could attend. They focused initially on sharing information on what people did: that is, what their expertise was. This initial trust-building was important in breaking down entrenched tribal barriers and meant that the meetings became springboards for other linkages between practitioners. One practitioner who supported a very successful local network explained her strategy:

'I think the very first step is understanding what the sort of issues are … Professionals have very, very different ideas about need, about discipline, about responsibility, about the impact of social systems on families … So I think the first step is to get some shared understanding about effective practices and about understanding the reasons behind some of them.'

This strategy also means that practitioners needed to be explicit about their own expertise. That expertise may be clearer in child protection work where statutory guidance leaves little room for manoeuvre, but may require some reflection when working in collaboration with others on prevention work.

Looking outward beyond professional boundaries

After a while, the focus in these meetings shifted to talking about relatively complex cases. These were not formal case conferences, but were examples of cases where individual practitioners thought they might get some help or advice from the collective wisdom of the meeting. This sharing of problems and expertise then led to what we described as new trails being cut in the local landscape, as, for example, where a troubled asylum-seeking child was helped to join a local football club, or a teacher learnt how to access family support as well as focusing on a child's difficulties. Talking about the success of these new trails helped practitioners to look outwards, beyond their professional boundaries to what others could offer. We began to see a shift in mindset among the practitioners, which valued these linkages and which built them in to their view of being a practitioner. One practitioner gave us her view of that shift and what she was learning from those meetings:

'It's about understanding at a deeper level. It's about connections. Maybe you are not sure about the child we are thinking about. But as we talk it through there may be a connection and if not for that child, maybe for another.'

From the parents' perspective this way of working was long overdue, as one parent told us during an NECF workshop with practitioners and parents:

'Can I just say something from a user's point of view as well – that if all the groups are sort of talking to each other and knowing what each other does – then if someone goes to one of the groups and they say "but this is what's going on in my life" and then they identify the support needs – and then they say "well we can do this part of it, but this project is going to deal with this part better than we could, this is our specialism, that's their specialism", that's really going to help the users.'

Key lessons for organisations

The lessons from the new networks we saw develop through the Children's Fund included the following.

- It was important to take time to develop trust and make informal links; for example, sharing mobile phone numbers proved very helpful.
- Practitioners learnt to be clear about what they could and could not offer and why. Focusing on specific examples helped people explore an increasing range of possible responses and to think in quite creative ways about working together for prevention.
- Discussions helped people to develop a mindset that looked outwards from their own professional bases to recognise what others could do.

These lessons take us towards thinking in more detail about practice. Encouragingly, once the practitioners started to reflect on what was involved, it did not seem too difficult. One practitioner explained what was involved as follows: 'Multi-professional work is only a matter of adjusting what you do to other people's strengths and needs.' However, we know from our current project, which is focusing directly on the organisational arrangements for interprofessional collaboration, it is very difficult for individual practitioners to adjust their practices to work responsively with other professionals, particularly if it involves taking shortcuts and bending the rules in their home organisations. For that reason we would stress that interprofessional practice cannot be regarded as the brave work of a few hero-innovators: it needs to be embedded in the principles and practices of each service if it is to work and organisations will need to change to accommodate it.

Implications for practice

Maintaining your own expertise

From what we have said so far it should be clear that we are suggesting that the specific expertise of each practitioner is important in interprofessional work. It is therefore crucial that children and families workers keep firm footholds in their professional base. This is important for two reasons. First, the access to regular supervision should not be ignored. It ties practitioners into the values and purposes of the profession and gives the kind of support that cannot be found elsewhere. Second, it helps to keep some perspective on the demands being made on their expertise. In one of the schools where we have worked, a social worker had just been employed. This worker was meant to be the school's salvation: '[Name] is going to be based in the school and this is a dream come true … we're absolutely cock-a-hoop.' However, in response, the social worker's supervisor was quick to point to the need for a common purpose: that is, that the children and families' perspective needed to be brought into the task to be undertaken: 'I think we have all got to work out what the common purpose of the work we do together is.'

It is also sensible for workers to maintain a foothold in their home organisation because it helps to retain a focus on what matters for the profession. Working on prevention does not mean that workers lose sight of the whole range of problems that might arise if early signs of vulnerability are ignored. Children and families specialists bring particular insights to interprofessional collaborations that are based on their being able to look down the line to see the longer-term implications of immediate decisions. They know better than any other profession the different thresholds and the actions they call for. They are not leaving the profession in order to play at prevention. Quite the reverse, they are bringing their knowledge of heavy end work to inform early decisions about a child's trajectory.

Both of our research projects have shown us that focusing on a child's trajectory, that is, on how a child is negotiating their way in the world, is the key to interprofessional work. It is something that all practitioners have in common: all would agree that they are working on strengthening the wellbeing of children. There are several implications of this approach. It allows all practitioners to put a child's interests first and to orchestrate their support to meet the child's needs. There may be times when it is sensible that the school is the main source of support and other times when the family worker's priorities are crucial. It particularly prevents practitioners from seeing that child as a set of 'bits' that are passed from service to service. Practice Example 1 presents an example of fluid and responsive collaboration.

Practice Example 1

An example of fluid and responsive collaboration

Twelve-year-old Jack arrived at school on Monday unkempt without his uniform and school bag and obviously in distress, although he was unwilling to talk to anyone at school. His form tutor, Jean, and the head of year (that is, the pastoral lead for that year group), Frances, had been keeping an eye on him for the previous two weeks as he had been arriving late, some homework had not been done and his uniform had often been incomplete. They had agreed that if this behaviour continued they would need to work on new behaviour targets with him. That Monday morning, having seen Jack, Frances tried to contact Jack's mother but could not reach her. Frances's records did not show that the family had been allocated a social worker; however, she was so concerned about Jack's withdrawn manner and obvious distress that she rang Luke, who was a member of the local social work team and whom she knew, in case there was a family worker involved.

Fortunately, Luke knew Jack's family and was working with them. He contacted Jack's mother and discovered that Jack's father had turned up out of the blue and demanded to take Jack with him now he was 12. Jack did not know his father and did not want to leave his mother, grandmother and two younger brothers. His father was staying at the family home and Jack had left home, and gone to stay with his grandmother on the other side of town. He was scared of his father as he had seen him being violent towards his mother when he was younger. There was no time for a case meeting as these took a minimum of three weeks to set up. Action was needed and Luke took it. He arranged for Jack to stay with his grandmother until his father left, took him to meet his father and to agree some contact, arranged some counselling for him and kept regular contact with Jack's mother. He also contacted the primary school attended by Jack's younger brothers to warn them of the situation.

Jean and Frances welcomed Jack whenever he was able to attend while staying with his grandmother and working things out with his father. They told all the teachers who worked with Jack that he would not be attending regularly and would not be doing homework. They also arranged for catch-up tutoring support for when he did return.

Luke agreed that he would discuss with his team how to let the head of the pastoral system in the school know when children in that school were part of his team's caseload. The head of the pastoral team felt that knowledge would help with the kind of quick response that Luke had been able to make.

Knowing how to know who

This fluid and responsive way of working calls for some new skills. We have already suggested that the meetings we saw during NECF helped practitioners to look outwards and recognise how others might support the children they were working with. We have called this skill 'knowing how to know who' (Edwards, in press). It is quite a complex skill. It involves being able to recognise what other practitioners can contribute to enhancing a child's wellbeing, knowing where that expertise can be found, knowing how to access it and then how to align one's own practices with those of other experts to support the child. This kind of work has also been described in more theoretical terms as 'relational agency' (Edwards, 2005). The argument there is that working in relation to other practitioners enhances the professional agency or capability of welfare practitioners who otherwise might find themselves quite exposed while working in flexible and responsive ways with vulnerable children and families.

Developing mutual respect

Knowing how to know who and the collaboration that follows also calls for practitioners to be professionally multilingual. We have already noticed that 'inclusion' has a history of meaning 'access to the curriculum' in schools. There are also obvious differences in the meanings and purposes of words like 'assessment' and different thresholds for what might be seen as inappropriate behaviour. Multilingualism, therefore, includes respecting the cultures of other professions. Several of the practitioners we interviewed during NECF were critical of how teachers worked with children and were pleased that children reported that they preferred to be in the after-school club or enjoyed being taken seriously by the family worker in ways that did not happen at school. We are not arguing that it is good educational practice to not take a child seriously, but that the practices to be found in schools have long histories and, as we have already argued, are sometimes beyond the scope of individual teachers to change. However, we are fairly confident that one outcome of increased interprofessional work with schools will be a return to a more child-centred approach and more of a focus on working from the child's perspective.

Understanding assessments in schools

Let us now move on briefly to assessment. Two forms of assessment are familiar in schools: assessment of academic performance and assessment of special educational needs. The latter involves a school's Special Educational Needs Co-ordinator and ultimately an educational psychologist who is attached to the school. In its early stages, an assessment of needs can lead to additional support from within a school and if this proves to be insufficient to meet those needs it can trigger a statement of educational needs authorised by the educational psychologist, which will bring with it additional resources. Schools therefore have well-established systems for identifying educational needs and for creating what may be called personal development plans or personal education plans for individual children, which are focused on their behaviour and performance in schools.

We have observed some anxiety among teachers about how these assessment ladders and personal plans, which are geared at including children in what the school offers, connect with the Common Assessment Frameworks that are crucial to integrated working in children and families services. At the time of writing it is too early to predict the outcome of the negotiations that are occurring across England. Instead we suggest that it would be wise to be alert to the purposes and importance of the assessment of special needs in schools.

However, once common assessment of some kind becomes embedded as part of interprofessional practice it will be important to know how to use it in the best interests of children. Our research has already begun to show that it can be used in a variety of ways. These range from using it in a fairly bureaucratic way, a form of 'ticking the box', to being the opportunity to include the child and family in the process by involving them in identifying goals and ways forward. We would suggest that the second option is the better one. It also takes us to the final implication for practice arising out of interprofessional work with schools: working in partnership with children and families.

Working in partnership with children and families

We noted earlier that the emphasis on curriculum in schools has meant that home–school relations have been dominated by school concerns. Schools, and particularly secondary schools, have a lot of ground to make up in their work with parents (Vincent and Tomlinson, 1997; Reay, 2001). There are, of course, examples of schools that have worked on developing links with their pupils' families, but it is not often a priority.

However, conversations with parents and practitioners in NECF showed how eager parents were to work alongside practitioners, to look forward and plan how to ensure that their child avoided a route to social exclusion. One Children's Fund practitioner explained how she and her colleagues were involving children and families:

> '... the main participation is in the individual packages we do with families, which are very much family-led really. It's around their description of the understanding of their needs – the targets that we all agree to work towards, and their evaluations of the things at the end really.'

The involvement of families in both setting targets and evaluating whether they had been achieved is clearly very powerful. It echoes Taylor's (1977) definition of individual agency, which proposes that we are only truly in control of our lives when we not only set our own goals but are also able to evaluate that we have achieved them.

Parents responded with enthusiasm to being treated as partners in working on their own child's trajectory in Children's Fund services. Talking of how she and her 13-year-old son worked with a family support worker, one mother explained: 'All three of us have worked together. I'm not told you do this, try that. It's "what do you think we should do?"'. Another described how she worked with workers at a project for excluded children attended by her sons: 'They talk to you, involve you, so you feel as though you're involved, they will ring your phone, actually talk to you, tell you what's going on, ask advice.' Children and families workers have given more thought to working with families to strengthen their capacities than teachers ever have. It is outside teachers' remit and is a major social work contribution to be made to supporting the wellbeing of children.

Key lessons for practice

This takes us to some other common attributes or skills in the systems of distributed expertise that we have been describing:

- Interprofessional work involves tolerance as well as trust.
- It involves helping other professionals see why working in a certain way with a child and family is important at a particular time.
- It also involves listening to them when they ask you to support their strategies at another time.

- Being flexible and responsive to children, families and other practitioners is crucial.
- That flexibility involves being confident about one's own expertise.

Trigger questions

➲ What could the expertise of social workers contribute to education settings?

➲ What might be the challenges facing social workers when working more closely with teachers?

➲ What might be the possibilities of collaborative working with teachers?

Recommended resources

➲ The Teacher Development Agency (TDA) has the responsibility for the development of extended schools. Its website provides useful information on how the English government is supporting the development of these arrangements: www.tda.gov.uk/

➲ Again in England, www.hm-treasury.gov.uk offers a range of useful publications arising from the Treasury's lengthy review of services for children and families.

➲ In the US, a programme called 'No Child Left Behind' was inaugurated by President Bush in 2001. The federal government's website is www.ed.gov/nclb/landing.jhtml. The programme remains controversial.

Note

[1] The two projects are: (i) the National Evaluation of the Children's Fund (2003–06), a DfES-commissioned evaluation of the Children's Fund, which runs from 2000 to 2008 and aims at preventing the social exclusion of children and young people aged 5–13 through partnership work and encouraging participation in service development;

and (ii) an ESRC-TLRP Phase III study of learning in and for interprofessional work (2004–07). The TLRP team includes the authors and Steve Brown, Harry Daniels, Jane Leadbetter, Deirdre Martin, David Middleton and Paul Warmington.

References

Cabinet Office (2006) *Reaching Out: An Action Plan on Social Exclusion*, London: Cabinet Office.

Clemens, S., Kinnaird, R., Mackey, T., Deakin, G. and Ullman, A. (2005) *Extended Services in Schools: Baseline Survey of Maintained Schools*, RB 681, London: DfES.

Cummings, C., Dyson, A. and Todd, L. (2004) *Evaluation of Extended Schools Pathfinder Projects*, RB 530, London: DfES.

DEMOS (2004) *Schools Out: Can Teachers, Social Workers and Health Staff Learn to Work Together?*, London: DEMOS-Hay.

DfES (Department for Education and Skills) (2004) *Every Child Matters: Change for Children*, London: DfES.

DfES (2005) *Extended Schools: Access to Opportunities and Services to All: A Prospectus*, London: DfES.

DfES (2006a) *Working Together to Safeguard Children: A Guide to Inter-agency Working to Safeguard and Promote the Welfare of Children*, London: DfES.

DfES (2006b) *Parenting Support: Guidance for Local Authorities in England*, London: DfES.

DH (Department of Health) (2004) *National Service Framework for Children, Young People and Maternity Services*, London: DH.

Edwards, A. (2001) 'Researching pedagogy: a sociocultural agenda', *Pedagogy, Culture and Society*, vol 9, no 2, pp 161–86.

Edwards, A. (2005) 'Relational agency: learning to be a resourceful practitioner', *International Journal of Educational Research*, vol 43, no 3, pp 168–82.

Edwards, A. (in press) 'Learning how to know who: professional learning for expansive practice between organisations', in S. Ludvigsen, A. Lund and R. Saljo (eds) *Learning in Social Practices: ICT and New Artifacts – Transformation of Social and Cultural Practices*, Oxford: Pergamon.

Edwards, A. and Warin, J. (1999) 'Parental involvement in raising pupils' achievement in primary schools: why bother?', *Oxford Review of Education*, vol 25, no 3, pp 325–41.

Edwards, A., Barnes, M., Plewis, I. and Morris, K. et al (2006) *Working to Prevent the Social Exclusion of Children and Young People: Final Lessons from the National Evaluation of the Children's Fund*, RR 734, London: DfES.

Evans, P. (1995) *Our Children at Risk*, Paris: OECD.

Home Office (2000) *Report of Policy Action Team 12: Young People*, London: Home Office.

Jack, G. (2006) 'The area and community components of children's well-being', *Children and Society*, vol 20, no 5, pp 334-47.

Moll, L. and Greenberg, G. (1990) 'Creating zones of possibility: combining social contexts for instruction', in L. Moll (ed) *Vygotsky and Education: Instructional Implications and Applications of Sociohistorical Psychology*, Cambridge: Cambridge University Press, pp 319-48.

Moran, P. and Ghate, D. (2005) 'The effectiveness of parenting support', *Children and Society*, vol 19, no 4, pp 329-36.

Nias, J. (1990) *Primary Teachers Talking: A Study of Teaching as Work*, London: Routledge.

OECD (Organisation for Economic Co-operation and Development) (1998) *Co-ordinating Services for Children and Youth at Risk: A World View*, Paris: OECD.

Reay, D. (2001) 'Finding or losing yourself: working class relationships to education', *Journal of Education Policy*, vol 16, no 4, pp 333-46.

Taylor, C. (1977) 'What is human agency?', in T. Mischel (ed) *The Self: Psychological and Philosophical Issues*, Oxford: Oxford University Press, pp 103-35.

Vincent, C. and Tomlinson, S. (1997) 'Home–school relationships: the swarming of disciplinary mechanisms', *British Educational Research Journal*, vol 23, no 3, pp 361-77.

Accessing and using multi-agency services: the experience of families

Leonie Jordan

Introduction

This chapter examines the experiences of parents who either seek services or are required to use services because there are safety and protection concerns about their child. The term 'parent' is used to include any person who is bringing up a child, not just a parent with 'parental responsibility', and the term 'family' embraces a wide range of arrangements in which children grow up (1989 Children Act, section 17(10)). Within this context the chapter explores the challenges for child welfare professionals and their agencies charged with responsibility for providing 'joined-up' support services. These experiences are located in the legal framework for family support services and in the wider context of the tensions between the government policy for family support services as set out in the Every Child Matters agenda (see www.everychildmatters.gov.uk) and the day-to-day reality for both families and professionals. The chapter concludes with seeking to match what families find helpful with suggestions about how we can improve multi-agency professional relationships with families.

Families generally want what is best for their children. This is evidenced by parents seeking information and advice from both statutory and voluntary agencies, as well as from informal networks. The government's current family policy (the Change for Children agenda) accepts the need and responsibility for providing mainstream health and education services but also recognises that some children and their families will need at various times additional support services. For families, the challenge is to get the services they need in a timely way from the range of agencies responsible. Families want to work in partnership with professionals to achieve the best possible outcome for their child and want to be able to choose and to be 'in control' of the services provided for their child (Quinton, 2004).

Despite government policies that state clearly the importance of supporting families, and research that shows that family support both benefits and protects children, the reality for many families is that services are not available until crisis point – often the point at which there are child protection concerns, exclusion from education provision or intervention through the criminal youth justice system. The irony is that neglecting to identify and support families experiencing difficulties when the problems are emerging may result in the child being removed into the care of the state at much greater cost to the child and their family, and ultimately to society (HM Treasury and DfES, 2007).

What are the experiences of parents when seeking support services?

A central characteristic of support is that it 'involves both a giver and a receiver' (Quinton, 2004, p 21): the mere accounting of what kind of support is provided does not suffice when considering how professionals can assist families. Any discussion of what may be useful has to take into account the experiences of the person receiving or using the support.

The Family Policy Alliance is a partnership of the Family Rights Group, the Family Welfare Association and Parentline Plus, three voluntary agencies who provide information, advice and advocacy for families and who work together to influence family and social care policies. Part of an initiative undertaken by the Alliance in 2004 was to find out from families involved in the partner organisations their views about using both voluntary and statutory (local authority) services. The following is a brief summary of the findings; the quotes come directly from family members who contributed to the consultation. The themes and issues identified resonate with the findings from the work of Ghate and Hazel (2002).

Fears of stigma and failure

Families are concerned that if they ask for help, if they say they are struggling or they do not know what to do, then they will be labelled as failing. They fear that their children may be removed from them. They therefore say they tend to seek assistance outside the family network only when crisis point is reached. They feel that parenting is a private matter and moreover that the government and child welfare professionals are critical of them. Asking for help, they believe, is not seen as a sign of strength but rather as failure. These perceptions present a considerable barrier for professionals and agencies responsible for providing services.

> 'I don't want to ask for help for many issues about being a parent because of the fear of being labelled a bad parent.'

Parents also talk about how they feel disloyal to their children and the family if they talk about problems and seek help. Although research (Ghate and Hazel, 2002) indicates that parents tend to seek advice and support from informal networks before turning to more formal sources, Parentline Plus consultations with parents show that they are hesitant to talk about problems outside the immediate family. For some parents, family and friends networks are limited, not safe or non-existent, for example where a parent has had to move to a different location because of domestic violence or to improve employment opportunities.

> 'Our family life is ours alone. It's private whatever the problems. Sometimes we talk to our family or maybe a friend who is in the same boat, but a lot gets unsaid.'

What makes services effective?

Support services are only effective if they are provided in a way that is welcomed rather than resented by families. Achieving this is challenging, particularly if there are child protection concerns – situations where often in reality the family has very limited choice about whether they will use the services provided.

Family feedback suggests that effective services depend on two factors:

- Parents need to be listened to when they say what would be useful to help them bring up their children, and their knowledge about their family and their children needs to be respected.
- Professionals need to support families to find their own solutions to the challenges that parenting a child may be presenting, working with the family's strengths to establish a partnership that makes clear what is being provided, by which agency, for how long and how they can review and renegotiate the services provided. In terms of multi-agency services, families are concerned about the whole package of services, not about how agencies will sort it out between them.

Quinton (2004, p 83) summarised parents' aspirations as:

Parents wanted services

- To treat them like adults
- As partners in problem solving
- To be practical and professional
- To take their needs seriously
- To be fast and responsive.

A mismatch between what is offered and what is wanted

Equally important is often the mismatch between services that parents say they would have found useful and what they actually received on the basis of professional assessments of what would benefit the child and what services might be available. The survey completed by Buchanan et al (2002) of parents receiving services in one local authority supports this: the parents of school-aged children who were users of local authority services identified support with depression (38%), an opportunity to meet other parents in the same position (32%) and counselling (33%) as being the most sought-after services from a 'wish list' of 24 services. Two thirds in their view did not have their needs met. Instead the services on offer from the local authority were parenting advice and support, one-to-one work with children and help with children's behaviour. At first sight these services may seem useful but parents did not perceive them as such given their assessments of their own needs. Rigid professional preconceptions about what the family needs and demarcation between services for the children and services for the parents are not helpful when constructing an effective child-centred partnership with the parents. A recent literature review exploring whole family approaches reinforces the concerns about professional boundaries negatively impacting outcomes for children and for families (Morris et al, 2007).

Listening, not telling

Research into family support services tends to focus on attempts to establish how effective various types of interventions are in achieving predefined outcomes for children (Moran et al, 2004). There is a tendency for professionals to tell families what their problems are and what will be provided to assist them, rather than listening to what families have to say and working with them to find services across agencies and sectors – statutory, voluntary and private – that they consider to be useful. This tendency is reinforced by government policy, which prevaricates between a commitment to support, acknowledging the challenges of parenting, and – particularly in youth justice and some aspects of education policy – an approach that is based on perceived shortcomings on the part of parents to raise their children adequately (Gillies, 2003).

The studies reviewed by Quinton (2004) confirm that parents need to feel in control of and responsible for solving problems for their children, with help if necessary from service providers. Parents are more likely to welcome support from a person who can directly understand their experiences, for example in dealing with supporting a child making the transition from primary to secondary school, and thus have a preference for less formal sources of advice and support. Research indicates that parents appreciate parenting and information-sharing programmes led by those who have gone through similar experiences (Grimshaw and McGuire, 1998). A later study by Gillies and Edwards (2003) found that more than three quarters of over 1,100 parents interviewed preferred family and friends as the sources of advice and support. Parents did, however, see a role for the state in providing material help such as financial support if necessary and access to housing.

Such views by parents do not necessarily minimise the skills that professionals have to assist families. Often initial information or support from informal or voluntary agency networks can lead to a more effective and confident use of statutory services through self-referral. However, these views do pose a challenge for service providers – they indicate the need for responsive flexible provision, something that demands skilful inter-agency working.

The legal framework for family support services

1989 Children Act, Part III

The general duty on local authorities to provide support services is contained in Part III of the 1989 Children Act. An important decision interpreting the provisions in section 17(1) (see Box 5.1) was made by the House of Lords (*R (on application of G) v Barnet London Borough Council, R (on application of W) v Lambeth London Borough Council, R (on application of A) v Lambeth Borough Council* [2003] UKHL 57, [2003] 1 All ER 97) considering three appeals made on behalf of children about whether, when the local authority had identified a particular need as part of an assessment of a child, it was under a duty to provide that service or resource to the individual child. A majority of the House of Lords decided that the duty under section 17 was a 'general' duty owed to all children who were 'in need' in the area of the local authority. This duty was targeted to all children generally who have additional needs [children 'in need'] as defined in section 17(10) and (11) of the Act. These needs are beyond those provided for by universal education and health services. The House of Lords said that the duty owed to an individual child or family was limited, which means that neither the child nor the family can require the local authority to provide services. Thus, even if the child and their family are assessed and meet the 'in need' criteria, they may not get the additional support services they consider would be useful.

BOX 5.1: *The 1989 Children Act*

Section 17(1) – the general duty of local authorities

(1) It shall be the general duty of every local authority (in addition to the other duties imposed on them by this Part) –

   (a)   to safeguard and promote the welfare of children within their area who are in need; and

   (b)   so far is consistent with that duty, to promote the upbringing of such children by their families,

by providing a range and level of services appropriate to those children's needs.

The Act uses a broad definition of 'family' to include any person caring for a child, and services can be provided either directly to the child or to the person caring for the child provided this is to the child's benefit. The Act then sets out a range of support services for children 'in need', which includes disabled children, primarily aimed at promoting the wellbeing of children. The local authority has considerable discretion about the extent of the support services it will provide or commission from other agencies such as the voluntary or third sector.

This lack of power on the part of a child or parents to require the local authority to provide services has resulted in a number of agencies working with families to recommend that the law be amended to entitle a family to have an assessment of their child's needs at their instigation rather than relying on the local authority to agree to 'do' the assessment. Not only would this enable families to 'self-assess', it would also enable the local authority to fulfil more effectively its duty to identify the levels of need in its area and to plan service provision with other agencies (Family Policy Alliance, 2005a, 2005b).

Aldgate and Statham's (2001) overview of the government-funded studies examining the implementation of the 1989 Children Act concluded that preventative services as envisaged in Part III of the Act are provided in 'a climate of intense competition for resources for public welfare services' (p 141) with the inevitable outcome that services targeted to children 'in need' tended to be directed towards the most needy children and, even more so, to children at risk of 'significant harm'.

This finding reflects the experience not only of families but also child welfare professionals, who are often frustrated by the limitations on both the kinds of services available and the duration of services given to an individual child. Many families will need continuing services to provide stability for their children, not just short-term provision. Professionals may find that to obtain services for a child there has to be a high level of concern about 'harm', with the child being made subject to child protection enquiries, leading to a child protection conference and child protection plan (1989 Children Act, section 47; DfES, 2006a).

In practice, the state struggles with the fierce competition for allocating public funds between the universal services of health and education and the competition for funds between social care support services and services for children at risk of harm. Because the consequences of failure to protect children from abuse and harm appear in the short term more immediate, the tendency is for resources to be absorbed by acute need at the expense of sustained funding of preventative services.

2004 Children Act, sections 10 and 11

Reflecting the growing concern not only that resources were directed more to child protection services than to preventative and support services but also that there were weaknesses at strategic and operational levels about how professionals jointly supported children and their families, the government established requirements for inter-agency collaboration in the 2004 Children Act. Under sections 10 and 11 of this Act, the Director of Children's Services is accountable for collaborative partnerships across agencies involved with the wellbeing of children to assist professionals to coordinate services focused on prevention and early intervention and, where appropriate, to plan and develop joint services.

To deliver these partnerships in practice the government has provided guidance on using tools such as the Common Assessment Framework (DCSF, 2007) to enable professionals from the differing agencies to work across professional boundaries, sharing common approaches to working with families to identify needs a child may have for additional or specialist services. In addition, the government is developing the 'Lead Professional' concept whereby when children are identified as having additional or specialist needs that require a range of supports, one among the group of professionals involved with the family will be expected to take on a case-coordinating and, to some extent, advocacy role for the child and family in relation to service provision (DCSF, 2007).

1998 Human Rights Act and non-discriminatory services

Overarching both the 1989 and the 2004 Children Acts is the 1998 Human Rights Act (see Box 5.2), which requires agencies with responsibilities for child health, education and welfare services to comply with the requirements of the European Convention on Human Rights. Of particular relevance is Article 8 – respect for private and family life. This Article does not give an absolute guarantee to family life and therefore to services to support a family to bring up their children. It is a 'qualified' right, and the state and its agencies have to balance the child's entitlement to grow up cared for by their family, who may need support services to do so, against the duty to protect the child and, where necessary following a fair and transparent process, to remove the child from the family.

BOX 5.2: *1998 Human Rights Act*

This Act applies the rights contained in the European Convention on Human Rights to law passed by the UK Parliament and includes duties on the state:

- to respect family life and private life [Article 8];
- to secure the right to life [Article 2];
- to protect citizens from inhuman or degrading treatment and torture [Article 3];
- to ensure security and liberty [Article 5];
- to provide the right to a fair hearing if civil or criminal charges are made by the state [Article 6];
- to protect from forms of discrimination [Article 14].

Discrimination legislation includes:

- 1975 Sex Discrimination Act;
- 1976 Race Relations Act;
- 1995 Disability Discrimination Act.

Legislation can be found on www.legislation.hmso.gov.uk/acts.htm

For a more detailed discussion on the impact of the 1998 Human Rights Act and discrimination law and related case law see Brayne and Carr (2005).

BOX 5.3: *International treaties*

International treaties creating obligations on the state include:

- 1989 United Nations Convention on the Rights of the Child, see www.unicef.org
- 1950 European Convention on Human Rights and Fundamental Freedoms, see www.coe.int

The duty on the Director of Children's Services to plan with other agencies to commission and provide support services to promote children's wellbeing must comply with both international obligations and domestic law to ensure that service provision is non–discriminatory. The legislation and Conventions create the framework for delivering these responsibilities: it is professionals working with children and their families who are the interpreters and decision makers as to how services to enhance the wellbeing of children are developed and delivered, as well as acting as the gatekeepers to resources.

The law in practice

Families frequently find that the threshold to meet the criteria for accessing services is set so high that they have reached crisis point before an assessment of the child's needs is carried out. A child who may have benefited from some additional supports may well either miss out on services until a critical decline in the parents' capacity to care triggers an assessment to access services. Agencies likewise may have no shared understanding of where and how that threshold is set.

As the parent described in Practice Example 1 so tellingly explains, she felt compelled to take drastic steps to bring her difficulties to the local authority's attention, only to find that their response was to begin child protection enquiries.

Practice Example 1

Difficulties in getting support

One of the parents whom the Family Policy Alliance interviewed (and who had also contacted one of the partner organisations' helplines) talked about the behaviour of her 10-year-old son – his aggression made the family home unsafe for her and his two siblings. She had sought help through his school, which had referred her to the Child and Adolescent Mental Health Services (CAMHS) and also the local authority. At the same time the school was also threatening to suspend her son. Her doctor considered that it was Children's Services' responsibility to take the first steps and that he could not refer her son to CAMHS without the support of a social worker. Children's Services believed that the matter was better dealt with as part of the school's actions. The mother assumed that the agencies had talked to each other. Professionals in each agency thought it was another agency's responsibility to assist the mother. Reaching a low point, this parent did not collect her son from school one day, aware that this was a high-risk step, but she hoped that this would trigger a response from one of the agencies. It did, but in the form of a child protection response, involving not only the local authority but also the police.

'I was horrified when I realised what I had done. I had put all of my children at risk of being taken away because I was seen as a single mother who could not cope. The social worker told me that the best way to get help was to agree to my son's name being put on their list of children who were being harmed [the child protection register]. I did not think this was fair for my son or me or my family. What I wanted was some help, not a label which his school and my doctor then found out about.'

The current policy debate

In March 2007, the government published a review of family policy resulting from an extensive consultation with providers of services, young people and parents to lay the foundation for government spending over a three-year cycle from 2008 (HM Treasury and DfES, 2007). As part of the Every Child Matters agenda, the government is aiming to address the imbalance in the allocation of resources between prevention services and protection services and also to develop a more effective multidisciplinary framework of professional skills to enhance the effectiveness of prevention services.

Two broad aims are to develop the resilience of children to adverse factors in their family and social circumstances and also to address the needs of families 'caught in a cycle of low attainment'. The goal is to increase the provision of 'preventative' services but where necessary to require resistant families to use the services by setting consequences for parents through forms of Anti-social Behaviour Orders and Parenting Orders. The intention is to enable local authorities to use additional funding flexibly to develop services provided either directly by the local authority or through multidisciplinary settings such as 'extended school' services or children's centres for younger children.

The policy review commissioned four areas of 'sub-review':

- developing preventative approaches;
- children and families at risk through 'low attainment';
- needs of disabled children;
- needs of young people.

These policy aims will inform not only funding streams to local authorities, child health and education but also expectations about workforce skills developments (see www.hm-treasury.gov.uk).

What does this mean for professional practice?

The Family Policy Alliance as part of a project to find out what families wanted from professional services worked with them to draw up a list. The following is what families from various parenting programmes, shared support groups and community-based projects told us. The voices of fathers were not as available as we had hoped – an issue that the government has recognised in its recent Policy Review.

Parents' messages

DO

- Give us reliable information about services from all the agencies.
- When we ask, assess our children's needs and direct us to the right services.
- Organise services for the family's convenience, not for professionals'.
- Seek our ideas for solutions to problems.
- Make us confident that our children are safe and happy when using the services.
- Respect our culture and value our skills.
- Check with us what works in our family and keep on checking because situations change.
- Be honest: tell us if our children are at risk and why, so we can work with professionals to make them safe.
- Tell us when you are sharing information about us and our children with other professionals.

DON'T

- Assume you know what is best for our family and override our own culture and traditions.
- Assume you know who is bringing our children up – it could be another family member.
- Make us feel ashamed about asking for help – listen, respect us and help us solve the problem.
- Pass us on from one agency to the next so we have to keep repeating what the problem is.

These messages should not come as a surprise to professionals. Professional systems and managers should aim to integrate these expectations into the values of the individual practitioner and the organisation in which they work. Multidisciplinary agreements to provide services need to reflect a shared agreement about the principles on which the professional partnerships are built.

What do the messages mean?

Informed by the messages directly from families, from various forms of service user consultation with families, children and young people and from research, there are significant implications for multi-agency practice.

At senior management level

The principles for joint commissioning and delivery of services must be explicit both for families and for practitioners working across agencies. Both need to know how decision making about service provision is carried out, how reviews of services are made and how to make representations if services are either not satisfactory or not provided. Both families and professionals need to know that they will not be punished for seeking as far as practicable the right services for the child. Imaginative arrangements to provide a wide range of providers using children's centres, extended school provision and other third sector agencies to deliver multidisciplinary services must be developed and expanded. Service users need to be properly consulted in the planning of services and their delivery and senior managers need to be better informed of effective ways of consulting with service users.

At operational management level

Managers need to support staff to have the time necessary to listen to the family to build mutually trusting partnerships and explore what services may be useful. If we expect social workers or the lead professional to be an advocate for the child and family, we need to accept that they may have a different view from that of a manager or resource panel. Operational managers need to help build confident cross-agency relationships within which practitioners and families can map out the services a child may need.

At practitioner level

Multi-agency frameworks for practice need to connect with the whole network of a child or family – and develop a practice that is family focused and child centred.

If we look again at the situation the parent talking to the Family Policy Alliance found herself in (see Practice Example 1), we can see that by the time professionals became involved this parent was distressed, anxious and doubtful about welcoming any professional to talk to her about her concerns.

The school staff may have focused too narrowly on the 10-year-old boy as a pupil – one who was not achieving in the classroom, who was likely to be disruptive and, because of his behaviour, a risk to other children. They did not necessarily have either the knowledge or the confidence to refer the parent to local voluntary services. The suggestion that she contact the local authority children's services made her feel that she was seen as failing and that she was the problem. If this mother had been signposted to a helpline or support group she may have felt less isolated, listened to and able to find solutions to manage her son's behaviour. Parent-to-parent services supported through training and peer support are an effective way of enhancing community capacity and regeneration:

> 'Talking to another parent made so much difference. It seems OK to be miserable and worried when someone else knows exactly what you are talking about.'

Because the mother had no entitlement to an assessment from children's services she could not begin the process of seeing if her son was considered to be a child 'in need'. The busy social care team considered that the real issue was the boy's behaviour in school and did not act upon the mother's self-referral.

None of the professionals involved with the mother or the boy talked to each other; each thought it was someone else's responsibility to initiate steps to respond to the mother, with the end result being that the boy was 'catapulted' into the child protection system.

What skills does a social worker need to assist families to access multi-agency services?

- Families say that they value the social worker who helps them find their solutions to family problems. This approach takes into account service users' anxieties about sharing family information with professionals and harnesses the family's strengths to build self-confidence and more sustained solutions. The whole family approach — family focused and child centred — is central to working with children and their families in a multi-agency setting. Social workers bring a broad knowledge and skills base and are able to move beyond functions into solutions — they need to influence those other agencies surrounding the child to adopt a more collaborative strength-based approach.

- An approach that respects the family but does not condone the behaviour towards the child or the child's behaviour is likely to enable the family to respond to early intervention and to take up services offered rather than being driven to use the services by compulsion. However, social workers cannot at times avoid compulsion — through either a child protection plan or court proceedings. Families need to know what sanctions may follow if there are serious concerns about a child that they do not address. Communication about options and consequences from the outset of intervention is central to good practice. Such clear communication is also needed for other agencies that may be involved — families and children should not need to repeatedly share with professionals from different settings the difficulties they are experiencing.

- A key skill social workers bring to their practice is the capacity to understand the issues from the family's standpoint. Social workers need to take into account the impact of poverty, social marginalisation, discrimination and poor health on parenting capacity and children's development. Social workers are the bridge to enabling other professionals to acknowledge the need for services and their responsibility to provide suitable services.

- Social workers need to have a sound knowledge of the third sector services available in the locality and how to support families to obtain these services. Beyond this, social workers need to understand the skills entailed in forming partnerships with these organisations to deliver effective services. For some families signposting to community resources will be adequate; however, some families may need the social worker to advocate access to these services on their behalf. Social workers will need to help other agencies to recognise and value services that may be community based and developed in response to discrimination.

- Clear communication is a prerequisite to establishing good partnerships with children and young people, the family and the professionals involved. Work needs to be planned around time to listen, time to reflect and time to establish relationships with the child or young person and the parents at a pace that works for them.

- Communication means not only using language that families understand, so that terms familiar to professionals are properly explained and examples given, it also means establishing in what way they wish to share information. This principle needs to be embedded in the practice of all the professionals delivering services to the families. Some families may wish to use an appropriately skilled interpreter. Some may want to share with the social worker the task of making written records or completing assessment forms. Other families may feel unable to say that written records disenfranchise them because of limited literacy skills.

- The boundaries on information recording and sharing both within the family and with other professionals need to be made clear at the outset. When sharing information with the family and other professionals it must be clear what are agreed facts, what facts may be in dispute, what the analysis is based on and how the conclusion was reached. There needs to be an open mind when listening to families: avoid stereotyping or making assumptions about the skills of other professionals involved with the family. Sound knowledge of local information–sharing guidelines is essential (DfES, 2006b).

- Social workers in multidisciplinary work may take on the role of advocate for the child and family to persuade other agencies to deliver services. When doing so it is essential to understand the nature of the advocate's role and be clear about any tension between the child and the parent's needs for services and the consequences for the child's wellbeing if services are not available.

- Disagreements may arise between the child or young person and the parents or other family members as well as professionals. The social worker needs to be confident about recognising disagreement and using their skills to find consensus and also assessing the risk that disagreement may pose to the child and the family. Early naming and bringing out into the open differences of professional viewpoints is often the responsibility of the social worker and it is for managers to find solutions and make decisions about what action to take.

- Services plans should be transparent and should clearly set out which agencies are involved, what is being provided, for how long and what are the consequences of not using the services. Plans need to be reviewed regularly and families need to know who has responsibility in multi-agency plans to deal with disagreement, to account for lapses in service provision and to ensure that reviews are held.

Conclusion

For families the government's proposals under the Every Child Matters agenda create the possibility of improvements in accessing services across agencies. However, joint planning and commissioning will only be effective if parents, families and children are consulted about what services are useful to them. Services delivered through extended schools and children's centres need to be innovative and harness the skills of the third sector to deliver not only universal services but also services for children with additional and specialist needs.

Social workers and their managers are well placed to drive forward more effective ways of working directly with families: the risk is that processes designed to ensure accountability will create unnecessary barriers for skilled professionals who want to work alongside families to support them to find solutions.

'Parents sometimes need help – we shouldn't be afraid to ask someone to listen to us.'

Trigger questions

➲ To what extent can and should families guide multi-agency responses to their needs?

➲ What might be the key barriers to multi-agency working when a child is in need of support rather than protection?

➲ What are the particular messages for social work practice when supporting multi-agency working in services to black and minority ethnic communities?

Recommended resources

⊃   The Family Rights Group produces various family guides, advice sheets, briefings and policy documents. It also offers a free telephone advice service, www.frg.org.uk

⊃   Parentline Plus offers information and support for families and professionals and a free helpline. It publishes relevant advice and training material and a series of policy documents, www.parentlineplus.org.uk

⊃   ATD Fourth World works to eradicate poverty and provides support to individuals and to organisations, www.atd-uk.org

⊃   The National Academy for Parenting Practitioners aims to support practitioners working with parents through the development of research, sharing knowledge and influencing policy and practice, www.parentingacademy.org

References

Aldgate, J. and Statham, J. (2001) *The Children Act Now: Messages from Research*, London: Department of Health.

Brayne, H. and Carr, H. (2005) *Law for Social Workers* (9th edition), Oxford: Oxford University Press.

Buchanan, A., Ritchie, C. and Bream, V. (2002) *Wiltshire Family Services Study 2001: The Views of Families who are in Contact with Social Services*, London Barnardo's.

DCSF (2007) *Common Assessment Framework: Practitioners' and Managers' Guides*, www.everychildmatters.gov.uk.

DfES (2006a) *Working Together to Safeguard Children: A Guide to Inter-agency Working to Safeguard and Promote the Welfare of Children*, London: DfES.

DfES (2006b) *Information Sharing: A Practitioner's Guide*, London: DfES.

Family Policy Alliance (2005a) *Parent Participation: Improving Services for Children and Families*, London: Parentline Plus.

Family Policy Alliance (2005b) *Supporting Children and Families*, Briefing Paper, London: Parentline Plus.

Ghate, D. and Hazel, N. (2002) *Parenting in Poor Environments: Stress, Support and Coping*, London: Jessica Kingsley Publishers.

Gillies, V. and Edwards, R. (2003) *Support for Parenting: The View of Parents of 8-12 year old children, who were asked about Sources of Support for Parenting,* Bulletin No 2, Families and Social Capital ESRC Research Group, London: South Bank University.

Grimshaw, R. and McGuire, C. (1998) *Evaluating Parenting Programmes: A Study of Stakeholders' Views,* London: National Children's Bureau/Joseph Rowntree Foundation.

HM Treasury and DfES (Department for Education and Skills) (2007) *Aiming High for Children: Supporting Families,* www.hm-treasury.gov.uk

Moran, P., Ghate, D. and van der Merwe, A. (2004) *What Works in Parenting Support? A Review of International Evidence,* DfES Brief No RB574, London: DfES.

Morris, K., Hughes, N., Clarke, H., Tew, J., Mason, P., Galvani, S., Lewis, P., Becker, S., Burford, G. and Loveless, L. (2007) *Whole Family Approaches: A Review of the Literature,* London: SEU.

Quinton, D. (2004) *Supporting Parents: Messages from Research* London: Department of Health/Jessica Kingsley Publishers.

Making sense of social work practice in multi-agency mental health services

Ann Davis, Alex Davis and Tony Glynn

Introduction

> I saw the psychiatrist every three months if well and two weeks if unwell. At the day centre the social worker introduced me to anger management groups, confidence building groups, they were a spring board for going out and about, teaching about life skills. I found this very helpful.

> No one told me anything. My social worker and support worker stopped coming and didn't tell my tenancy support worker and me anything. Then they left and I was told I wouldn't get any support, but they had done nothing. It's no wonder I told them they were useless. (Brannelly and Davis, 2006, p 13)

These two service user accounts, of the contrasting responses made by mental health practitioners to periods of crisis in their lives, highlight the importance of good multi-agency practice in the mental health services. The first service user experienced a variety of responses to what she needed following her discharge from psychiatric hospital. Her sense of recovery was promoted by her use of a range of inputs, and her social worker played a key role in accessing these opportunities for her. The second service user was discharged from hospital into supported accommodation. The practitioners involved in his care felt that this environment would assist him in managing the enduring mental health problems he experienced. However, on discharge he found himself facing considerable difficulties in making this major life transition because the practitioners who knew him withdrew their support.

In both of these accounts the role of the social worker was identified by the service users as key to the way in which they were able to live their lives following a mental health crisis. As Clare Allan, mental health service user and award-winning novelist, describes it,

In my experience, the relationship between client and social worker has the potential to be the most helpful intervention of all. Mental health problems seldom stem from a single cause. Too often, those on the medical side are blinded by diagnosis, too ready to reach for a tidy biological explanation. But people are always much more than mere biology. Working as they do in the midst of the mess, social workers can help us make sense of ourselves, not only as individuals, but as part of the society that made us the people we are. (*The Guardian Society*, 1 August 2007, p 2)

Every social worker, whatever their specialist area, will find themselves working with people who have mental health problems. Evidence shows that mental distress is strongly associated with the kind of social and economic disadvantage that characterises the profiles of the majority of people in contact with social workers (ODPM, 2004; Davis, 2007). The isolation, social exclusion, poverty, poor health, unemployment, inadequate housing and debt that people using social work services experience increase their vulnerability to mental distress.

Some social workers choose to work with people who have a diagnosis of mental ill-health. This kind of social work has been shaped by changes in mental health policy and practice as well as the changing relationships between social care and health services. Since the 1980s the contraction and closure of old psychiatric hospitals in the UK has resulted in an increasing number of community-based mental health services being established (Bell and Lindley, 2005). Reflecting this change, mental health social workers are employed in (or seconded to) the primary health, specialist health, social service, voluntary and independent sectors. Many, although not all, are part of what are called multidisciplinary mental health teams – working alongside psychiatrists, nurses, occupational therapists, psychologists and a range of support workers to meet the needs of people with a psychiatric diagnosis. Increasingly these teams, particularly in urban areas, are providing specialist functions such as assertive outreach and home treatment/crisis resolution (Onyett, 2005).

From this variety of locations social workers are expected to respond to individuals in mental health crisis and with long-term needs. They offer individuals and their family members counselling, advice, support and guidance and advocate and negotiate for them in relation to difficult but important issues in their lives such as accommodation, treatment options, transport, income, employment and access to leisure activities (Gilbert, 2003).

In addition, a minority of social workers in the UK undergo post-qualifying specialist training to acquire legal powers to assess individuals for compulsory admission to hospital. Only one other country outside of the UK – Malta – has created such a role for mental health social workers. These social workers were called Approved Social Workers (ASWs; now AMHPs – see below) in England, Wales and Northern Ireland and Mental Health Officers (MHOs) in Scotland. In England, for example, they have to be registered with the General Social Care Council (GSCC), have completed an appropriate programme of post-qualifying training and been approved by their social services authority as ASWs/AMHPs. In using the powers conferred on them, they have been involved, with psychiatrists and general practitioners (GPs), in assessing the need for individuals to be compulsorily admitted to hospital – referred to as 'sectioning' (for more details, see Brown, 2006).

The 2007 Mental Health Act has now opened up this area of specialist work in England and Wales to other mental health practitioners. The title Approved Mental Health Professional (AMHP) has replaced that of ASW. At the same time local authorities and the GSCC have retained their responsibilities for approving, training and registering a range of mental health professionals, including social workers.

In considering social work practice in multi-agency mental health services, this chapter provides:

- an overview of the complex and changing legal and policy contexts of mental health services and their impact on social work practice;
- a brief review of the relevant research literature;
- a consideration of the key challenges and opportunities facing social workers working in multi-agency mental health services;
- ways of developing and sustaining creative mental health social work that is informed by the needs of service users and the realities of multi-agency working.

BOX 6.1: *Glossary of terms used*	
AMHP	Approved Mental Health Professional
ASW	Approved Social Worker
CPA	Care Programme Approach
GP	general practitioner
GSCC	General Social Care Council
MHO	Mental Health Officer

Legal and policy contexts

Tracking the shifting locations of social work in mental health services over time is a complex task. This is largely because responses to national mental health policy and the use of the funding available for service provision is increasingly a matter of local decisions made by the health and social care sectors. These decisions have resulted in the involvement of a range of mental health service providers spanning the statutory, voluntary and independent sectors. The resulting diversity in operational and organisational arrangements makes it impossible to make anything but general statements about what multi-agency work means for mental health social work practice across the UK and within each nation.

So, to provide an example of how recent changes in the legal and policy context have impacted on mental health social work, we list in Box 6.2 the key elements of the legal and policy context of multi-agency working in mental health in England. We then briefly discuss each in relation to their impact on mental health social work practice. Those students and practitioners who wish to generate an equivalent list for Northern Ireland, Scotland and Wales should use the following resources: Bamford, 2005; Atkinson, 2006; DH website, www.dh.gov.uk. In doing this they will spot some strong similarities and interesting differences with England.

BOX 6.2: *Legal and policy context of multi-agency working in mental health (England)*

1975   *Better Services for the Mentally Ill* White Paper (DHSS, 1975)

1983   Mental Health Act

1990   NHS and Community Care Act

1991   Care Programme Approach

1995   *Building Bridges: A Guide to Arrangements for Interagency Working for the Care and Protection of Severely Mentally Ill People* (DH, 1995)

1998   *Modernising Mental Health Services: Safe, Sound and Supportive* (DH, 1998)

1999   *National Service Framework for Mental Health: Modern Standards and Service Models* (DH, 1999a)

1999   *Co-ordinating Care: The Care Programme Approach and Care Management* (DH, 1999b)

1999   Health Act

2001   Health and Social Care Act

2001   *The Journey to Recovery: The Government's Vision of Mental Health Care*
(DH, 2001a)

2001   *Safety First: Five-year Report of the National Confidential Inquiry into
Suicide and Homicide by People with Mental Illness* (DH, 2001b)

2007   Mental Health Act

While mental ill-health is recognised as a major global health issue, with around one in four adults estimated to experience mental illness during their lifetime, it has always occupied an under-resourced and marginal position within the UK health services as well as local authority adult services, where the focus is primarily on the social care needs of older people. Disputes about what constitutes social need and health need among people with mental health problems play a prominent and often divisive role in decision making about the allocation of health and social care services.

It was the introduction of a range of state-provided services in the late 1940s that laid the basis for a major change in mental health service provision in the UK. Universal social security benefits, public housing, free healthcare, particularly from primary care services, and the recruitment of social workers to local authority services as well as the NHS, provided the foundation for dismantling the Victorian legacy of the asylum/hospital system that had segregated people with mental health difficulties from the mainstream. Despite the declaration by the Minister of Health in the early 1960s that the time had come for the 'elimination of by far the greater part of the country's mental hospitals' (Powell, 1961), no adequate legal or funding framework was put in place to deliver the range of community-based alternatives that could make adequate alternative provision for people with mental health problems.

In 1975 the *Better Services for the Mentally Ill* White Paper (DHSS, 1975) delivered a vision of what a community-based service for people with mental health problems in England and Wales should look like as psychiatric hospitals closed. Health, social services and the voluntary sectors were expected to work together. Their mission was to develop coherent and accessible local services that would provide opportunities for people to live within the community while receiving support, guidance and treatment for their mental distress.

It was acknowledged that a barrier to achieving this vision lay in the fact that most of the government's investment in mental health services was tied up in psychiatric hospital services. Additional investment together with a redirection of existing investment was needed. But the White Paper appeared at a time when government was dealing with the impact of a worldwide oil crisis, negotiating International Monetary Fund loans and rising unemployment. Welfare cuts rather than increased investment were the order of the day and so the growth of alternative provision in the mental health field was slow. However, the adverse economic pressures did trigger the closure of psychiatric hospitals.

At this time most mental health social workers were employed in local authority generic social work teams from which they worked in the community as well as being placed in mental health hospitals and clinics. But the changing policy agenda meant that they began to be offered opportunities to use their knowledge and skills in other settings. The first community mental health centre, designed to meet the needs of people with a diagnosis of mental ill-health in a local setting housing a multidisciplinary team, opened in England in 1977. By 1987 there were 54 of these health-funded centres and by 1997, 75 (Bartlett and Sandiland, 2007).

Following the 1983 Mental Health Act many social services departments began to reorganise their specialist mental health social work staff. Psychiatric hospital social work teams disappeared as hospitals contracted and closed. At the same time mental health social workers in generic adult service teams found themselves being moved to social services specialist teams. Mental illness or mental health social work teams were created, covering the increasing range of health and social care community settings. This meant that those social workers who decided to work in health-funded, multidisciplinary, community-based teams also had a social work team base and the associated supervision and management to relate to.

The 1990 NHS and Community Care Act brought to this complex territory of mental health social work delivery in England the procedures and processes of care management. At the same time the health service-led Care Programme Approach (CPA) was introduced. The rationale of the CPA was to coordinate service responses so that vulnerable (and possibly dangerous) individuals did not fall through the gaps of a complex health and social care mental health service system. The lack of a coordinated introduction of these initiatives was indicative of the ways in which the two key statutory agencies, tasked to deliver mental health services, were failing at national and local level to work together.

By the mid-1990s the integration of these two systems of need assessment was being urged, with an emphasis on meeting the needs of those diagnosed as having severe mental ill-health (DH, 1995). In 2001 integration was compulsorily imposed via a two-tier system of CPA – standard and enhanced. Mental health social workers have not played a key role in this system. It is generally health colleagues – community psychiatric nurses and occupational therapists – who become care coordinators. Evidence suggests that the model that has evolved operates as a bureaucratic means of resource rationing rather than as a way of making decisions about what is needed to support the lives and choices of service users (Schneider, 1999; Cambridge et al, 2005).

New Labour's modernising agenda for public services identified mental health services as 'a poor relation' (DH, 2001c). The levels of finance and the standards of both health and social care provision were described as inadequate for the task in hand. The *Modernising Mental Health Services* and *National Service Framework for Mental Health* documents (DH, 1998, 1999) provided a rationale and framework for change. Those working in, and using, mental health services noted that in this fresh formulation of purpose the development of good-quality, flexible and responsive community-based services were linked to an acknowledgement of the need to challenge the stigma, discrimination and social exclusion faced by people with a mental health diagnosis. This brought to the fore issues of the rights and entitlements of those experiencing mental distress, these connected strongly to the core concerns of social workers and service user activists (Barnes and Bowl, 2001; Campbell, 2005).

As these new opportunities were emerging another element in the mental health policy context was marking out mental health as a very distinct territory for social workers compared to other areas of the adult services. The 1980s and 1990s witnessed growing media and political attention being paid to what were perceived to be the dangers of mental health community care provision. These concerns focused on a small number of tragic incidents in which individuals in mental distress had attacked and killed other people. They were used to point up the dangerousness of people with a psychiatric diagnosis and the threat they posed to public safety. They played a key role in shaping government proposals about the need to introduce new mental health legislation to replace the 1983 Mental Health Act (DH, 2001b). The 2007 Mental Health Act introduces the means of compulsorily assessing and treating people outside of hospital.

The available evidence indicates that people with a psychiatric diagnosis are less likely than others to attack and kill other people (Lester and Glasby, 2006). Yet concerns with the issue of risk and mental ill-health have played an increasingly dominant part in debates about the direction of mental health policy, provision and practice. An emphasis on risk assessment and risk minimisation has shaped practice, raising difficulties for those social work practitioners who view risk taking as part of making changes and who see their role as working with service users to support their recovery (Davis, 1994). A tension exists in mental health services around issues of choice, care, control and containment. It is a tension that can raise difficulties at times for service users and social workers working in partnership towards common objectives.

Legislation at the turn of the century to underpin modernisation – the 1999 Health Act and the 2001 Health and Social Care Act – has had a significant influence on the working locations of social workers. Section 31 of the 1999 Health Act enabled health and social services to pool funds, adopt lead commissioning with agreed delegation and integrate provision. Following this Act an increasing number of local authority social services departments seconded their mental health social work staff to Mental Health Trusts where social workers are often based in multidisciplinary teams, with health staff as managers. This shift towards the increasing placement of social workers in health locations was further encouraged when the 2001 Health and Social Care Act introduced Care Trusts – NHS bodies which in some places provide both health and social care services.

The legal, policy and organisational frameworks in which mental health social work is delivered is characterised by a multi-agency approach in which a health/medical perspective on mental distress is dominant. Despite considerable recent reorganisation, it remains an area that is characterised by 'gross under funding and role confusion' (Coppock and Hopton, 2000) rather than joint commitment and vision. Multi-agency working has always been part of the context in which mental health social workers practise. However, the legal and organisational changes that have taken place over the last 20 or so years have resulted in a major shift of the location of mental health social workers from a statutory social care/social work base to a health base. Research about the impact of this change suggests that many mental health social workers are finding that they are faced with considerable challenges in relation to the organisational cultures in which they find themselves working; in particular the way in which they are managed and supervised by the health managers, who do not always recognise, value and support the social work knowledge, skills and values that they bring to mental health services.

Relevant research literature

The research literature that helps to make sense of social work in multi-agency mental health services covers three topics:

- partnership working between social care and health organisations;
- mental health social workers' views and experiences of multi-agency working;
- service users' and carers' views of the contribution that mental health social work can make to their lives.

Partnership working

The term 'partnership' is the term most frequently used when consideration is given to the ways in which agencies and practitioners are expected to work collaboratively in delivering mental health services. It is a term that encapsulates the key challenges and opportunities that are facing mental health social workers.

The Sainsbury Centre for Mental Health's work on partnerships suggests that:

> In mental health, partnership is of particular importance because its absence can lead to problems in communication and the co-ordination of care. Services need to be arranged around the user's needs and not around bureaucratic boundaries and incentives. (SCMH, 2000, p 6)

Reasons for promoting good inter-agency partnerships in mental health are that:

- Mental health is a complex area involving a wide range of very different agencies.
- Mental health is an area of scarce resources and broad tasks; it is therefore important for all to work together to achieve a vision of what is needed.
- Mental health service users are at times vulnerable and have limited capacity for negotiating the complex bureaucracies that contribute to their care so they need services that join up in a coherent way for them. (SCMH, 2000, pp 2-3)

Lester and Glasby (2006) in their chapter 'Partnership Working' provide a very useful overview of the research literature on this topic. It is a literature that is far from robust. It tends to ignore service user and carer perspectives, focuses on good rather than poor practice and often makes unevidenced claims about the benefits of partnership working. Despite these gaps, the literature is useful in identifying some of the benefits and barriers associated with partnership working.

The benefits include:

- the pooling of expertise among practitioners and managers;
- increased creativity in problem solving;
- a single point of contact for service users.

The barriers include:

- practitioners' lack of knowledge of the roles of those they need to work with;
- practitioners' lack of certainty about their own roles and their tendency to stereotype other workers;
- problems of engaging GPs and psychologists in partnership working;
- problems in relation to working with psychiatrists who take the view that multidisciplinary teams must be led by doctors;
- difficulties in recognising the importance of extending partnerships to include agencies that can meet the needs of service users and carers in relation to issues such as housing, income, employment, transport and leisure.

Research that has focused on ways of realising these benefits and addressing the barriers has suggested that it is important to:

- clarify roles and strategies;
- explore relationships with actual and potential partners;
- develop understandings of cultural and organisational change;
- involve users and carers in developing and realising partnership working.

However, in their summary of this area of research the Sainsbury Centre for Mental Health suggests that as 'there are no "quick fixes" and no magic solutions to complex health and social problems' (SCMH, 2000, p 27), progress needs to be incrementally based and locally focused.

Mental health social workers' views

There has been little research about the views and experiences of social workers practising in multi-agency mental health services. Yet this is an area where practitioners have experienced a great deal of change and have found themselves managing tensions between a number of competing interests and priorities.

Huxley et al (2005) interviewed mental health social workers about the stress and pressures they face working in multidisciplinary teams. They found that practitioners identified a combination of factors that put pressure on them. These included a lack of basic resources to meet service users' needs, heavy workloads, the burden of paperwork to meet the requirements of duplicating administrative systems as well as the constant reorganisation of health and social care agencies. It was when social workers found that their contribution to mental health services was not valued by their employing organisations that stress was greatest. This experience of being undervalued was identified as the trigger for mental health social workers deciding to resign from their posts. This research also highlighted the factors that kept mental health social workers committed to their work. These were their 'professional commitment to the goals and values of the profession, to serve the users. They also value membership of multidisciplinary teams where this is a positive experience' (Huxley et al, 2005, p 1077). These conclusions, upheld by another recent study (Cree and Davis, 2006), suggest that two factors are key to mental health social workers maintaining the focus and direction they need in the complex, changing, under-resourced world of multi-agency mental health services. They are:

- the commitment of mental health social workers to a practice that promotes 'social change, problem solving in human relationships and the empowerment and liberation of people to enhance well being' (IFSW/IASS, 2000, p 1);
- an appreciation of and response to what service users and carers are saying about what they need from services to survive and thrive.

Service user views

What service users say they need from mental health services provides a consistent set of messages to social workers across the research literature. As the rationale for providing mental health services is one of making positive changes in the lives of those with mental health problems, this evidence provides a substantial resource on which social work practitioners can draw in developing their practice in multi-agency mental health services.

A study by MacDonald and Sheldon (1997) gathered evidence from mental health service users about their views of social workers in a London social services department. This study highlighted the social disadvantage shared by those diagnosed with a mental illness and the way in which this generated social and financial difficulties that they needed assistance with. The majority of those interviewed were very positive about what social workers offered them. In particular they valued the emotional support and reassurance they received, practical help and advocacy, the respect with which they were treated and the way social workers coordinated services to meet their needs (Macdonald and Sheldon, 1997).

A survey in Leeds of users' views of mental health services found that the vast majority of service users identified talking, listening and counselling as being the most valued of social work services, closely followed by advice and practical help with benefits problems (LMHU, 1997).

A decade later similar messages emerge from the literature-based overview provided by Beresford (2007) of users' perspectives on the changing roles and tasks of social work. In reviewing the messages that consistently emerge from research about service users' views and what service users say about what they value in social workers, Beresford suggests that there are three that are fundamental:

- *the social approach*: a way of working with individuals which locates the issues that they face in the social context of their lives (that is, the perspective described at the start of this chapter by Clare Allan);
- *relationship*: a way of working that places value on establishing a relationship through which trust and understanding can be built;
- *personal qualities*: a way of working which focuses on warmth, respect, being non-judgemental, listening and treating people as equals.

In addition, service users value social workers who:

- offer information, advice and advocacy about practical issues;
- help people negotiate with other agencies about problems with benefits and housing;
- provide counselling and emotional support;
- value the expertise of the service user (Beresford, 2007).

Key challenges and opportunities for mental health social workers

As this chapter has outlined, one of the most important contributions that social workers have to make to multi-agency mental health services is the social perspective they bring to an understanding of mental health (Tew, 2005). The relevance of this perspective has gained some recognition in the current policy emphasis on social inclusion, recovery and user involvement. However, in the health-led environments of mental health services it is often difficult to see social perspectives shaping practice.

In considering the partnerships that are important to multi-agency working, social workers must recognise that they cannot be restricted to those they make with the social care and health organisations that deliver mental health services. As the *Mental Health and Social Exclusion* report (ODPM, 2004) highlighted, many people with a psychiatric diagnosis face difficulties in relation to areas such as housing, employment, income, leisure and social activities, all of which may necessitate the active engagement of staff from housing associations, local authority housing, transport and leisure departments and the Department for Work and Pensions (ODPM, 2004).

So, there are two, interrelated spheres in which multi–agency partnership working is important if social workers are to make effective contributions to the lives of people with mental health problems. These are:

- the multidisciplinary partnership arrangements promoted between health and social care agencies at organisational, management and practitioner levels to deliver effective mental health services;
- the multi–agency communication and joint working required between mental health services and a range of other agencies that are vital to obtaining the resources essential to mental health and wellbeing, for example accommodation, social security and employment.

This is an extremely challenging task for mental health social workers based as they are in locations where health and social care organisations are struggling to establish effective partnership. Despite policy exhortations and shifts in legislation to promote partnership working, there are considerable organisational, financial and professional barriers that impede the delivery of the flexible and responsive services outlined in mental health policy and practice guidance. In addition, the social perspectives that social workers bring to their work with individuals diagnosed with mental ill–health are not driving the organisational cultures that they find themselves working in.

Developing and sustaining creative mental health social work

Making sense of multi–agency working as a mental health social work practitioner involves you in working out how to use your knowledge, values and skills in partnership with service users, despite the difficulties of the terrain in which you are located. Your starting point is building good relationships with service users and those that care and support them. In taking forward the concerns that they identify as being critical to their wellbeing and recovery, you need to identify and engage colleagues from other disciplines and agencies who can play a part in delivering on these concerns. As you do this you will need to prepare for questions being raised about whether what you are engaged in is compatible with what they consider is in the best interests of the service user concerned (see Glynn and Ansell, 2006).

At the start of this chapter we focused on some of the legal, organisational and policy issues that can make mental health social work a complex and difficult task. We suggested that those practitioners who have found ways of working creatively in this area have done so by being guided by a strong sense of their professional commitment and values at the heart of which are concerns to work holistically with service users. However, we have also highlighted the reasons why it could be difficult to sustain a course of action in the face of a lack of recognition, value and support for social approaches to practice in mental health services.

One way of combating this difficulty is for social work practitioners to locate their distinct approach to working with service users in the framework outlined in Box 6.3. It has been developed explicitly to promote the idea that there are core elements that lie at the heart of good mental health practice regardless of discipline differences. It has been developed as an approach that is responsive to service users' needs and one which can promote a strong foundation for modern multi–agency mental health services. It gives explicit recognition to the priorities that social workers give to valuing diversity, respecting individuals, working to strengths and recognising the expertise of service users.

BOX 6.3: *The 10 essential shared capabilities for mental health practice*

Working in partnership: developing and maintaining constructive working relationships with service users, carers, families, colleagues, lay people and wider community networks. Working positively with any tensions created by conflicts of interest or aspiration that may arise between the partners in care.

Respecting diversity: working in partnership with service users, carers, families and colleagues to provide care and interventions that not only make a positive difference but also do so in ways that respect and value diversity, including age, race, culture, disability, gender, spirituality and sexuality.

Practising ethically: recognising the rights and aspirations of service users and their families, acknowledging power differentials and minimising them whenever possible. Providing treatment and care that is accountable to service users, carers and mental health services. Creating, developing or maintaining valued social roles for people in the communities they come from.

Challenging inequality: addressing the causes and consequences of stigma, discrimination, social inequality and exclusion of service users, carers and mental health services. Creating, developing or maintaining valued social roles for people in the communities they come from.

Promoting recovery: working in partnership to provide care and treatment that enables service users to tackle mental health problems with hope and optimism and to work towards a valued lifestyle within and beyond the limits of any mental health problem.

Identifying people's needs and strengths: working in partnership to gather information to agree health and social care needs in the context of the preferred lifestyle and aspirations of service users, their families, carers and friends.

Providing service user-centred care: negotiating achievable and meaningful goals, primarily from the perspective of service users and their families. Influencing and seeking the means to achieve these goals and clarifying the responsibilities of the people who will provide any help that is needed, including systematically evaluating outcomes and achievements.

Making a difference: facilitating access to and delivering the best-quality, evidence-based, values-based health and social care interventions to meet the needs and aspirations of service users and their families and carers.

Promoting safety and positive risk taking: empowering the person to decide the level of risk they are prepared to take with their health and safety. This includes working with the tension between promoting safety and positive risk taking, including assessing and dealing with the possible risks for service users, carers, family members and the wider public.

Personal development and learning: keeping up to date with changes in practice and participating in lifelong learning, personal and professional development for oneself and colleagues through supervision, appraisal and reflective practice.

(*Source:* DH, 2004)

Trigger questions

➲ In the locality in which you are working as a student/social worker, where are the mental health social workers located and what are the needs of service users and their carers?

➲ Can you identify three key principles that you consider essential for sound partnership working with service users?

➲ How compatible are the Ten Essential Shared Capabilities with the knowledge, values and skills of social work?

Recommended resources

In addition to the references listed, the following websites will keep you up to date with relevant developments and debates:

➲ **Department of Health:** search under mental health for updates regarding legislation, policy and statistical data, www.dh.gov.uk

➲ **The Mental Health in Higher Education Project:** an interdisciplinary project designed to enhance learning and teaching about mental wellbeing and ill-health, www.mhhe.heacademy.ac.uk

➲ **The Sainsbury Centre for Mental Health:** a centre working to improve the quality of life for people with mental health problems by influencing policy and practice in mental health and related services, www.scmh.org.uk

➲ **The Social Perspectives Network:** a coalition of service users, survivors, carers, practitioners, policy makers, academics and students interested in how social factors both contribute to people becoming distressed and play a crucial part in promoting people's recovery, www.spn.org.uk

References

Atkinson, J. (2006) *Private and Public Protection: The Civil Mental Health Legislation*, Edinburgh: Dunedin Press.

Bamford, D. (2005) *The Review of Mental Health and Learning Disability (Northern Ireland): A Strategic Framework for Adult Mental Health Services*, Belfast: DHSSPS.

Barnes, M. and Bowl, R. (2001) *Taking over the Asylum: Empowerment and Mental Health*, Basingstoke: Palgrave.

Bartlett, P. and Sandiland, R. (2007) *Mental Health Law, Policy and Practice* (3rd edition), Oxford: Oxford University Press.

Bell, A. and Lindley, P. (eds) (2005) *Beyond the Water Towers: The Unfinished Revolution in Mental Health Services 1985–2005*, London: Sainsbury Centre for Mental Health.

Beresford, P. (2007) *The Changing Roles and Tasks of Social Work; from Service Users' Perspectives: A Literature Informed Discussion Paper*, London: Shaping our Lives.

Brannelly, T. and Davis, A. (2006) *Service Users' Experiences of Transitions through Mental Health Services*, Birmingham: University of Birmingham, downloadable from www.socialresearch.bham.ac.uk

Brown, R. (2006) *The Approved Social Worker's Guide to Mental Health Law*, Exeter: Learning Matters.

Cambridge, P., Carpenter, J., Forrester-Jones, R., Tate, A., Knapp, M., Beecham, J. and Hallam, A. (2005) 'The state of care management in learning disability and mental health services 12 years into community care', *British Journal of Social Work*, vol 35, no 7, pp 1039-62.

Campbell, P. (2005) 'From little acorns – the mental health service user movement', in A. Bell and P. Lindley (eds) *Beyond the Water Towers: The Unfinished Revolution in Mental Health Services 1985–2005*, London: Sainsbury Centre for Mental Health.

Coppock, V. and Hopton, J. (2000) *Critical Perspectives on Mental Health*, London: Routledge.

Cree, V. and Davis, A. (2006) *Voices from the Inside*, London: Routledge.

Davis, A. (1997) 'Risk work and mental health', in J. Pritchard and H. Kemshall (eds) *Good Practice in Risk Assessment and Risk Management*, London: Jessica Kingsley.

Davis, A. (2007) 'Structural approaches to social work', in J. Lishman (ed) *Handbook for Practice Learning in Social Work and Social Care: Knowledge and Theory*, London: Jessica Kingsley.

DH (Department of Health) (1995) *Building Bridges: A Guide to Arrangements for Interagency Working for the Care and Protection of Severely Mentally Ill People*, London: DH.

DH (1998) *Modernising Mental Health Services: Safe, Sound and Supportive*, London: DH.

DH (1999a) *National Service Framework for Mental Health: Modern Standards and Service Models*, London: DH.

DH (1999b) *Co-ordinating Care: The Care Programme Approach and Care Management*, London: DH.

DH (2001a) *The Journey to Recovery: The Government's Vision of Mental Health Care*, London: DH.

DH (2001b) *Safety First: Five-year Report of the National Confidential Inquiry into Suicide and Homicide by People with Mental Illness*, London: DH.

DH (2001c) *Making it Happen: A Guide to Mental Health Promotion*, London: DH.

DH (2004) *The Ten Essential Shared Capabilities: A Framework for the Whole Mental Health Workforce*, London: DH/NHSU/Sainsbury Centre/ NIMHE.

DHSS (Department of Health and Social Security) (1975) *Better Services for the Mentally Ill*, London: HMSO.

Gilbert, P. (2003) *The Value of Everything*, London: Russell House Publishing.

Glynn, T and Ansell, J. (2006) 'Survival and abuse: what we can learn from it', *Journal of Social Work Education*, vol 25, no 4, pp 418–28.

Guardian Society, The (2007) 'It's my life column', 1 August, p 2, also on website, www.spn.org.uk

Huxley, P., Evans, S., Gateley, C., Webber, M., Mears, A., Pajak, S., Kendall, T., Medina, J. and Katona, C. (2005) 'Stress and pressures in mental health social work: the worker speaks', *British Journal of Social Work*, vol 35, no 7, pp 1040–62.

IFSW/IASSW (International Federation of Social Workers/International Association of Schools of Social Work) (2000) *International Definition of Social Work*, www.ifsw.org

Lester, H. and Glasby, J. (2006) *Mental Health Policy and Practice*, Basingstoke: Palgrave Macmillan.

LMHU (Leeds Mental Health Unit) (1997) *'A Little More Time Too': A Consumer Survey of the Leeds Mental Health Social Work Services*, Leeds: Leeds Social Services Department.

Macdonald, G. and Sheldon, B. (1997) 'Community care services for the mentally ill: consumers' views', *International Journal of Social Psychiatry*, no 43, pp 56–63.

ODPM (Office of the Deputy Prime Minister) (2004) *Mental Health and Social Exclusion*, London: Social Exclusion Unit.

Onyett, S. (2005) 'Mental health teams: hitting the targets, missing the point?', in A. Bell and P. Lindley (eds) *Beyond the Water Towers: The Unfinished Revolution in Mental Health Services 1985–2005*, London: Sainsbury Centre for Mental Health.

Powell, E. (1961) Speech to the Annual Conference of the National Association of Mental Health (now MIND), 9 March, for full text see www.mdx.ac.uk/www/study/xpowell.htm

Schneider, J., Carpenter, J. and Brandon, T. (1999) 'Operation and organization of services for people with severe mental illness in the UK: a survey of the care programme approach', *British Journal of Psychiatry*, no 175, pp 422-5.

SCMH (Sainsbury Centre for Mental Health) (2000) *Taking your Partners: Using Opportunities for Inter Agency Partnership in Mental Health*, London: SCMH.

Tew, J. (ed) (2005) *Social Perspectives in Mental Health: Developing Social Models to Understand and Work with Mental Distress*, London: Jessica Kingsley.

Working together: responding to people with alcohol and drug problems

Sarah Galvani

Introduction

There is a huge amount of shame and stigma attached to *problematic* alcohol and drug use. Commonly used terms such as 'junkie', 'alcoholic' and 'addict' conjure up images that lead to people hiding their use, not seeking help, and living in fear that someone – their employer, family, doctor or social worker – will discover the truth. As a result, people will often only seek help when their problematic use reaches crisis point or when they are compelled to do so. This may be through formal compulsion, for example through court-ordered treatment, or informally, for example a partner threatening to leave.

Help for people with alcohol or drug problems is provided by a number of professionals and specialist staff. But people with substance problems rarely need help with just one problem. Many have a number of problems that precede, coincide with and/or result from their problematic substance use. These problems commonly include experiences of child abuse, domestic abuse, financial difficulties, housing problems, trouble with the police, family breakdown, loss of employment, and physical and mental health problems. No one professional can be an expert in all these things. No one agency can provide all the services that a person may need. Multi-agency working is therefore essential.

Recent years have seen growing political recognition of drug and alcohol problems and their negative impact on communities, families and individuals' wellbeing. While this is undoubtedly an important development, it has not been matched by an understanding of the role social work can play in working with people with substance problems and preventing future problems developing. This chapter will explore these issues further, beginning with an overview of what is meant by substance problems and how social work as a profession is placed to respond. It will briefly explore the policy framework for, and the historical context of, social work's relationship with substance use services. It will also identify the challenges and opportunities this presents for multi-agency working and how these have been met by some social work and substance use professionals.

BOX 7.1: *Glossary of terms used*	
CARAT	Counselling, Assessment, Referral, Advice and Throughcare
GSCC	General Social Care Council
ICP	Integrated Care Pathway
MNS	Multiple Needs Service
NTA	National Treatment Agency
PCT	Primary Care Trust
YOT	Youth Offending Team

Problematic substance use

There are many different reasons why people start using substances. For some it is about fun, risk taking and experimentation, for others it may be to cope with experiences of abuse and trauma. Unfortunately, there are no clear indicators that determine *who* will or will not develop problems with alcohol or drugs. Many people use alcohol and/or drugs without incurring any problems at all. However, research evidence shows that there are a number of risk factors associated with increased vulnerability to developing alcohol or drug problems. For children and young people, poverty and deprivation, anti-social peers and behaviour, being in trouble at school, parental substance use, peer substance use, poor family cohesion and discipline, and weak parental attitudes towards bad behaviour are among the risk factors for drug and alcohol problems (BMA, 2006; Dillon et al, 2007; Frisher et al, 2007). For adults, risk factors include experiences of abuse in childhood (Downs and Harrison, 1998; Bear et al, 2000), domestic violence and abuse in adulthood (Downs et al, 1993; Corbin et al, 2001), adolescent substance use (DeWit et al, 2000), mental ill-health (DH, 2002) and social deprivation (Rhodes et al, 2003). All these factors are common among people presenting to social work services. Thus there is a clear need for social workers to understand these links and to work in partnership with other professionals to effectively address people's substance-related needs.

As well as not knowing *who* will develop alcohol or drug problems, there are also no clear indicators about *when* a person might develop problems with their substance use. There is no particular *amount* of alcohol or drugs, or a particular *type* of alcohol or drug, that will indicate problematic use; it will vary from person to person. Some people can use large amounts and not experience problems, although prolonged heavy use is more likely to have some negative impact on their health at least. Others can use relatively small amounts of alcohol or drugs and experience problems. It is therefore important for social work intervention to be based on a clear understanding of whether the substance use is causing problems for the person and what those problems are rather than assuming that any substance use is automatically problematic.

Having a basic awareness of alcohol and drugs and having the knowledge and confidence to ask about substance use are increasingly important in all areas of social work practice. Specialist substance use knowledge is not a requirement, although it is essential that social workers know what specialist resources are available and what type of support they offer. The most common support offered is individual counselling. This is sometimes combined with medical supervision and prescribing through the person's general practitioner or psychiatrists linked to a specialist service. Other types of support and intervention include group work, for example therapeutic discussion groups or educational groups, and couples, families and children work. Knowing what is available locally is the first step to successful partnership working with both substance use professionals and the service user.

Partnership working: where are we now?

Regardless of the social worker's area of specialist practice, the underpinning legislation and key policy drivers have made multi-agency and partnership working central to their requirements. Without it the service user can end up running back and forth between different services, with each service ignorant of what the others are doing. At best this means services are working independently from each other, at worst it means their advice, support and goals may conflict. This disjointed way of working does not reflect a client-centred approach nor is it helpful in meeting the client's needs. Thus the need for multi-agency working between social work and substance use services is to develop a more streamlined and less fragmented approach to supporting people.

In the substance use field, a greater political recognition of drug use and its associated harms has been accompanied by a number of policy initiatives, including national alcohol and drug strategies (Home Office, 2002; Cabinet Office, 2004). Such policy initiatives have targeted all aspects of substance use services from commissioning to practice guidance and workforce development. Multi-agency working has also been emphasised repeatedly within these policy frameworks.

BOX 7.2: *Models of care*

The two main documents guiding the commissioning, structure and delivery of drug and alcohol services are:

- Models of Care for the Treatment of Alcohol Misusers (MoCAM) (DH, 2006); and
- Models of Care for the Treatment of Drug Misusers (Home Office, 2002; DH/Home Office, 2006).

Together with their predecessor, *Commissioning Standards* (Health Advisory Service, 2000), the need for partnerships at strategic and/or operational levels has been highlighted frequently.

In addition, practice guidance has emphasised the need for partnership or inter-agency working, as well as proposing joint protocols and multidisciplinary working. This is an important shift from the historically individualistic focus of substance use services and potentially provides a good opportunity for improved collaboration with social work and social care services.

BOX 7.3: *Care planning*

New developments within the substance use field have seen the introduction of *a care planning approach* as well as guidance on how to do it (NTA, 2006). *Integrated Care Pathways* (ICPs) have also been introduced (DH, 2006; DH/Home Office, 2006) to ensure that people presenting to substance use services who require a number of specialist services will receive a more streamlined and coordinated service response.

There is also more specific practice guidance that focuses on particular groups of people in need of substance use services, for example people with mental ill-health (DH, 2002; Adfam/Rethink, 2004), young people, children and families (Hogg, 1997; Kearney et al, 2003b; DfES et al, 2005) and people suffering from domestic abuse (Stella Project, 2004; Women's Aid, 2005a, 2005b). They stress the need for collaboration in order for people's more complex needs to be met by the professionals most able to support them.

Thus, the principle of multi-agency working is peppered throughout the key policy drivers for social work and substance use services. The key questions are:

- whether it is happening in practice; and
- to what extent the impact of partnership working between substance use services and social work agencies has been evaluated.

Evidence

It is clear that there are examples of good practice and solid partnerships between social services and substance use services (some of which this chapter will describe) but research evidence evaluating the effectiveness of such partnerships is hard to find.

The challenges of partnership working between substance use services and social care and health agencies have been highlighted in a number of studies. Cleaver et al (2006, p 6), in a study of child protection practices and procedures in cases involving parental substance problems, found that substance use services were 'not routinely involved in any stage of the child protection process'. Weaver et al (2002), in a study of collaboration between mental health and substance use services, concluded that the co-existence of substance use and mental ill-health was often not picked up by both services. In a study of a partnership between a Youth Offending Team (YOT) and substance use projects, Minkes et al (2005) found that there were particular tensions between the agencies over confidentiality, referral criteria and attitudes to enforcement. Harman and Paylor (2005) highlighted how CARAT (Counselling, Assessment, Referral, Advice and Throughcare) schemes designed to help drug-using prisoners make the transition from prison to the community ran into problems, primarily due to ineffective partnerships. There are many studies like these that conclude with the need for better multi-agency working and partnership practice (Jones et al, 2003; Powell et al, 2003; Altshuler, 2005) but very little evidence to say whether partnerships that do exist are working or not.

What the evidence *has* shown for many years is that substance use interventions work best when the individual has positive social support and when the environment around them feels stable (Azrin, 1976; Costello, 1980; Powell et al, 1998; Dobkin et al, 2002). In other words, if the professionals involved in supporting the person can work together to help the person maintain or achieve this stability, for example securing housing, maximising income or resolving legal issues, the greater the person's prospects of overcoming difficulties in their lives (Harrison, 1996; Barber, 2002; Guy and Harrison, 2003). There is also American and European data that shows that a case management approach and, by inference, a multi-agency approach have improved outcomes for people. These outcomes reflect lower levels of drug use, better retention in treatment and also better access to, and use of, supplementary services (see Vanderplasschen et al, 2006, for review).

To conclude, the policy frameworks for both social work and substance use services identify the need for multi-agency working. However, the rhetoric of partnership working needs to be transformed into a practical, workable, operational response. This response, in turn, needs to be evaluated in order to provide evidence-based support for the partnership principle.

Looking back

To encourage partnership working where previously there has been very little requires some reflection on the historical barriers to multi-agency approaches.

Political recognition

The main barrier would seem to be the lack of political acknowledgement that social workers and social services are at the front line of working with substance problems, not just health and criminal justice colleagues (Home Office, 2002; Cabinet Office, 2004). This lack of acknowledgement has had a negative effect in terms of recognising the need for social work education, training and service delivery to adequately engage with substance use issues.

Education and training

There is no requirement for qualifying social workers to learn about alcohol and drug use and relevant interventions on current social work programmes. Despite decades of debate and guidance on this subject (see Galvani, 2007, for review), there has been little response from social work educators (Forrester and Harwin, 2006; Galvani, 2007). One study has shown that the majority of training on substance use is provided by employers rather than through formal training processes (Galvani and Hughes, in preparation). This oversight appears to be a missed opportunity to improve the knowledge base of the next generation of social workers and stem the flow of social workers who lack the knowledge and confidence to work with these issues.

Service delivery

There are a number of barriers relating to service delivery:

Lack of mutual understanding

One of the requirements for effective multi-agency working is having some understanding of each other's roles and the priorities and procedural frameworks that underpin them. Evidence suggests that this has been lacking between social work and substance use services and has led to a mistrust of each other's practice and to defensiveness or overly sensitive concerns about, for example, sharing information (Kearney et al, 2003a; Cleaver et al, 2006; Forrester and Harwin, 2006). Staff fear that by disclosing information they will break agency confidentiality procedures or damage their therapeutic relationship.

Different professional philosophies

Many interventions for alcohol or drug problems use medical models of addiction with subsequent interventions based on that model. At a simplistic level, this model sees alcohol or drug problems as an illness or disease. The intervention is thus focused on abstinence from the substance use with the assumption that other problems will be addressed once there is no alcohol or drug use. Conversely, social work interventions are underpinned by social models of care that emphasise the role of social learning and the influence of environmental factors on human behaviour and development. They do not expect the multiplicity of people's problems to be resolved by focusing on one particular problem and as a result adopt a holistic approach to a person's needs.

Not my job

There has been a lack of recognition within the social work profession that substance use is an issue that cuts across all specialist areas of social work practice and one that social workers should be engaging with and addressing, even if only at a basic level (Lawson, 1994; Adams, 1999; Harwin and Forrester, 2002; Guy and Harrison, 2003; McCarthy and Galvani, 2004; Forrester and Harwin, 2006). People with substance problems are often viewed as being less deserving than other groups of service users due to a perception that such problems are self-inflicted, when the reality is that people with substance problems are often extremely vulnerable and using substances to cope with an array of problems.

Competing priorities

At the core of social work practice are a number of professional duties and legal powers. Whatever the social worker's specialism, the welfare of the child is paramount and takes precedence over other considerations. One criticism of social workers is that this focus on the child has failed to recognise that working with the parent's substance use can protect and help the child. On the other hand, at the heart of substance use services is the sacrosanct relationship between the specialist substance worker and their adult client. The key criticism is that this adult-only focus has been to the detriment of children (Cleaver et al, 2006), with some agencies not even asking whether the person has children and putting their therapeutic relationship ahead of the children's needs. This criticism was echoed in a review of 40 Serious Case Reviews (conducted when a child dies or is seriously injured through abuse or neglect) (Sinclair and Bullock, 2002). The review concluded that there was a need for more attention to women as mothers and not just as individual adults. However, it also recommended that social workers needed to be able to identify alcohol problems. This adult versus child polarisation has been demonstrated further by evidence that shows the lack of child protection referrals from substance use professionals (Forrester and Harwin, 2006) as well as the failure of social workers to 'consult or collaborate' with substance use services (Cleaver et al, 2006, p 10).

Looking forward

Political recognition

Although policy has largely overlooked social work's role in substance interventions and prevention, there is increasing recognition that social workers are among a range of professionals working in the community who could be better equipped to identify and address substance use among their client group. The Department of Health has clearly stated that health and social care staff should be able to conduct a basic assessment of a person's substance use, recognise signs and symptoms of substance use, gather information on related problems, identify any immediate risks and make appropriate referrals (DH, 2006b; DH/HO, 2006).

In addition, particular attention has been paid to social care and health staff working with parents, children and families, as evidence shows the need for better protection of children living with parental substance use (and often co-existent domestic abuse) and improved interventions with parents who have substance problems (Advisory Council on the Misuse of Drugs, 2003; Cleaver et al, 2006; Forrester and Harwin, 2006).

Education and training

Changing social work education to ensure that all newly qualifying social workers have an awareness of substance use and appropriate basic interventions would stem the flow of social workers entering practice with little or no preparation for working with alcohol or drug problems. This is unlikely to happen in the near future but there are some initiatives under way to improve education and training. The General Social Care Council (GSCC) and the Department of Health are currently co-chairing a strategic group, the Social Work and Substance Use Advisory Group, which brings together the key organisations involved in the training and development of the social work and social care workforce. In addition, the British Association of Social Workers, in collaboration with the University of Birmingham and Aquarius, is intending to launch a Special Interest Group for social workers wanting information and support on working with alcohol and drug issues.

There are also more self-directed learning opportunities available as a result of the investment in drug services and the development of its specialist workforce. There has been an increase in training materials, websites and training courses available to health and social care staff.

Service delivery

Lack of mutual understanding

A lack of understanding about the roles of other professionals can easily be overcome through better communication and joint learning and working arrangements. Without this communication and mutual understanding even informal working arrangements are unlikely to succeed.

The introduction of care planning frameworks and ICPs into the substance use field provides obvious opportunities to share knowledge and experience. Care planning frameworks have been embedded in social work practice for many years, primarily through the implementation of the 1990 National Health Service and Community Care Act. This shared knowledge should provide both social work and substance use staff with a common language and understanding of coordinated care that will facilitate better partnership working.

Different professional philosophies

Despite the apparent polarisation of medical and social models of care, there are an increasing number of substance use services using interventions based on social learning theories including motivational and cognitive behavioural techniques. These fit more closely with methods of working used in social work interventions and should allow for a better understanding of ways of working as well as providing social workers with transferable skills that can be used to complement substance use interventions. It is important that social workers have some understanding of medical models of substance use and related services in order to provide service users with an informed choice of services. For example, well-known self-help organisations such as AA (Alcoholics Anonymous) and NA (Narcotics Anonymous) are based on disease models of addiction and provide important 'out of hours' support for many people with alcohol or drug problems.

Not my job

There is very little research evidence on social workers' attitudes to working with people with substance problems and this is an obvious gap in the research. However, anecdotal evidence from frontline social workers, coupled with research within mainly children and families social work teams, demonstrate high levels of substance use problems among service users (Kearney et al, 2003a; Cleaver et al, 2006; Forrester and Harwin, 2006). The evidence further reveals that staff often do not know how to work with substance problems because of their lack of training on these issues. Some Local Safeguarding Children's Boards now have a chapter on working with parental substance use in their child protection procedures. However, an equivalent does not exist for social workers working with adult client groups. The recent recognition in the *Models of Care* documents (DH, 2006b; DH/HO, 2006) that social workers are among a number of frontline professionals working with people with substance problems should lead to greater levels of training and awareness. They call for regional drug treatment commissioners to make arrangements for training Tier 1 staff in order to support partnership working. This offers a step towards more informed practice and better collaboration.

Competing priorities

Competing priorities may always exist on some level but as the emphasis on supporting families and children affected by substance use increases, anecdotal evidence suggests that both substance use and social work services are becoming more aware of the need for improved collaborative working. In April 2007 the National Treatment Agency (NTA) introduced new datasets that required all drug treatment agencies to record the parental status of their service users as well as the number of children and pregnancy status for each service user (NTA, 2007). Whether this data translates to better frontline practice remains to be seen. There is also evidence of more family-oriented methods being adopted by some substance use agencies, for example Social Behaviour and Network Therapy (Copello et al, 2006).

In terms of social work provision, some qualified professionals may benefit from the revised post-qualifying award for people working with children, families and carers that now requires the inclusion of a number of areas of competence relating to substance use on its curriculum (GSCC, 2005).

To conclude, while there are barriers to partnership working there is also hope for better working relationships in the future as well as evidence that some agencies have managed to overcome these barriers, seemingly driven by innovative leadership and/or the commitment of frontline staff. The following section provides examples of both formal and informal partnership working arrangements.

Good practice

Kharicha et al (2004), in their review of this subject, concluded that there was little evidence that formal partnership arrangements were any more effective than informal ones. However, informal relationships formed at an individual level are more likely to fail as key individuals move on.

This section provides an overview of three main models of partnership working that currently operate between social work and substance use services, illustrated with examples from practice.

Collaborative working

Social work and substance use agencies remain separate in terms of their specialist areas of practice and physical location but work closely together to provide an informed and holistic service to their service users. Often the service users may be the same and the agencies will be collaborating on different aspects of the person's care to ensure that their work is complementary and supportive of the service user's needs.

Practice Example 1

Multiple Needs Service, CASA – London
Information supplied by James Lakey, Multiple Needs Counsellor

CASA provides a range of services to people needing support for their substance use. The Multiple Needs Service (MNS) was specifically set up for people experiencing mental ill-health and who are also using alcohol or illicit drugs. The main role of the service is to help people to stay in contact with mental health services where an alcohol or drug issue may be having a negative impact on their mental ill-health and their engagement with mental health services. The service works closely with the local Mental Health and Social Care NHS Trust, taking referrals from community psychiatric nurses and social workers based in the local Community Mental Health Teams. Following a referral, CASA staff will meet with the service user to begin the assessment process. This spans two sessions because of the holistic approach to assessment adopted by CASA. Between these two sessions, and during subsequent one-to-one work between CASA and the service user, the referring social worker or community psychiatric nurse and CASA staff keep in close contact to ensure that they are sharing information and providing mutual support. Service users are fully aware of the arrangement and the open confidentiality policy adopted by CASA.

The challenges
- Having enough time to talk properly to make sure the partnership works well.
- Confidentiality and sharing of information. Often the client does not feel comfortable about information sharing but an agreement is put in place at the start so that everyone is clear.
- Service users will sometimes tell different stories or different parts of it to the two professionals. This can potentially create conflict between the professionals about appropriate interventions if they are not aware it is happening.

The opportunities and benefits
- Mutual support of having another professional involved.
- Sharing of expertise and knowledge.

Embedded working

In this model, the social worker has received training in working with alcohol and drug issues and is therefore able to identify and address many substance use issues in the context of their work with the person or family without the need for specialist input from other services. Specialist support is only called for if the worker and service user identify that more intensive work on the substance use is needed, for example medical interventions including detoxification or in-patient residential rehabilitation.

Practice Example 2

Option 2 – Cardiff

www.option2.org
Written by Mark Hamer, Senior Practitioner/Therapist

Option 2 works with families in crisis where there are serious child protection concerns and parental substance misuse. It works to enable carers to adequately parent their children and move the children out of the 'child protection' arena and into a 'child in need' situation. This requires intensive one-to-one work with a holistic focus. This sometimes requires workers to be available seven days a week. We are trained to work in a solution-focused way with whatever issues the family presents to us, including alcohol and drug problems. Option 2 is part of the local authority adult services and is managed by a social services drug and alcohol manager. We take referrals only from childcare social workers and have informal arrangements to fast-track substance-misusing parents into specialist substance misuse services.

The challenges
- Cultural differences between different service areas can cause friction, for example child focus of children's services, adult focus of adult services and family focus of our service. Children's services particularly seem to find it difficult to understand that we will be looking at family functioning and looking at everybody's needs.
- Lack of experienced practitioners in childcare teams often leads to fearfulness, over-reaction and an unwillingness to work with risk.

- Children's services make the decision of who should be referred to Option 2. Therefore those families that are labelled as 'not engaging', who may benefit most from the model, may not be referred.

The opportunities and benefits
- Creating a bridge between adult and children's services, sharing of skills, understanding and resources with positive outcomes for children and families.
- The opportunity to work closely with the childcare teams and to influence the coordination of timely services to families.
- The opportunity for families to receive a seamless service, with a clear division between the policing role of childcare workers and the supporting, enabling role of our service.

Specialist workers or projects

There are four potential subgroups under this category:

(i)   *a social work team specialising in substance use* – this is most common in a local authority setting where teams of substance specialist social workers focus on helping people to access residential rehabilitation, in particular conducting the financial assessments, arranging the placement and allocating funding to it.

Practice Example 3

Hull City Council Social Services Department

Drug and Alcohol Service
Written by Lynne Froud, Senior Practitioner (Substance Misuse)

The Drug and Alcohol Service of Hull City Council is a social services team. We are informally integrated into the Hull Primary Care Trust (PCT) Addiction Service. This enables us as workers to have access to a person's medical information, database, clinical team, key workers and community psychiatric nurse (homeless team). Social services' specific role is to take on referrals for people who are seeking residential rehabilitation for their alcohol or drug problem and to complete the preparation, assessments and funding applications with close liaison with the PCT's Addiction Service. Social services do not act as key workers.

The challenges

■ Occasionally the culture of medical versus social models of working can become apparent and can cause some tensions, for instance: difference between the medical/social model and an understanding by clinical staff of social services' role and remit within the team.

■ There can also be professional differences and different approaches to treatment, but this is not always a negative thing.

The opportunities and benefits

■ Better communication, access to key workers and the clinical team.

■ Within the PCT Addiction Services there is access to an enormous resource of different experience and skills and training opportunities.

■ Integration into the PCT results in having access to inpatient facilities and being able to discuss issues at weekly team meetings – this makes the transition from inpatient detoxification to residential rehabilitation less complicated for the service user.

■ There is also an outreach worker who assists with engaging people into treatment. Sometimes this is all that is needed to help someone's motivation towards change.

(ii) *a multi-agency team delivering substance use services (among others)* – this can be referred to as a 'one-stop shop', where teams of different professionals work together to provide a holistic response to people's needs. This may include a social worker specialising in substance use or another area of social work, for example mental health, depending on the remit of the team.

(iii) *a specialist 'satellite' social worker* – this is where a social worker is placed within an alcohol or drug service to provide information and advice to the team and to jointly work with service users who need some specialist social work support (Kearney et al, 2003a).

(iv) *specialist focus projects* – these projects are set up to address substance use with a particular focus on a service user group. The social worker may be part of that team because they are specialists in the area in focus or because they specialise in substance use. In addition, some social workers will seek to specialise in drugs and alcohol and seek employment within voluntary or statutory sector drug and alcohol services, for example within a community alcohol or drugs team, or a specialist service run by a charitable organisation.

Practice Example 4

ru-ok?, Brighton and Hove
Written by Dan Caruana, Senior Social Worker

ru-ok? is a multidisciplinary substance misuse service (Tier 3) for young people, aged 10–19, in Brighton and Hove. The service adopts a harm reduction approach and supports young people to address difficulties at home, in education, training and employment and with other issues such as housing. We also aim to involve parents and carers in this work where desirable and helpful to the young person.

We have a number of different relations with social services at different levels. At a senior management level we are overseen by the manager of the local YOT, who in turn reports to the assistant director of children's services in the children's trust. On an operational level we have contact with the duty teams in the city, taking initial referrals from the public and professionals about child protection and children in need. We also have contact with the local leaving care team and local family support/long-term social work teams. These are informal arrangements.

The challenges
- Lack of understanding among social work teams about the structure of substance use services (there are four tiers of service and referrals need to be appropriately targeted).
- Helping people to understand the concept of harm reduction and that it applies equally to young people as well as adults.
- Having young people's substance use recognised as a child protection issue to the same degree as parental substance use.
- Encouraging social workers in these teams to routinely discuss substance use issues with the young people on their caseload.

The opportunities
- Keeps the issue of young people's substance misuse 'on the agenda'.
- Supporting colleagues to locate young people's substance misuse within the current Every Child Matters/Common Assessment Framework agendas, in a holistic way.
- Working together to produce practice guidance and establish accompanying training.
- Supporting social work colleagues to develop a more detailed knowledge of substance misuse issues generally among young people.

Conclusion

What these models and examples show are the ways services and practitioners are finding to work in partnership. They also provide evidence of the similarities in the challenges, opportunities and benefits presented by partnerships between social work and substance use services regardless of the model of partnership working that is adopted. They demonstrate that an important precursor is a willingness to communicate with each other and overcome organisational and professional obstacles, including a willingness to learn about each other's work culture, priorities and systems. Multi-agency working will remain a challenge until there is some level of shared understanding about commonalities, differences and the priorities of different disciplines and services.

The policy frameworks for both social work and substance use services demand multi-agency working; however, the historical relationship between substance use and social work professions suggests that barriers may still need to be overcome. There are examples of good practice at both formal and informal levels but there is a need for effective monitoring and evaluation of these partnerships, from both agency and service user perspectives, to prove that they result in a better, more holistic service for service users.

Politically and strategically, at both national and local levels, there needs to be greater recognition of social workers' role in working with people with substance problems. In the meantime, there are undoubtedly opportunities for individual staff to make a difference within social work and substance use services. There are improvements in practice and an increasing number of opportunities for improving partnerships between substance use and social work services. There are similarities in service delivery frameworks, increased training opportunities and resource availability, as well as an increasing recognition of the importance of addressing substance use within specialist areas of social work practice. In addition, social work training needs to include knowledge about alcohol and drug use as well as ensure that there is adequate reflection on the values and principles that underpin social work practice in relation to this service user group.

The greater the level of individual need, the greater the need for multi-agency working. People with alcohol and drug problems usually have a multiplicity of complex problems and vulnerabilities that need to be recognised and addressed by a holistic professional response.

Trigger questions

⮕ To what extent do the key policy drivers for social work and substance use services reflect the need for multi-agency working?

⮕ What are some of the benefits of joint working cited by agencies currently working in partnership?

⮕ What can you do on an individual and agency level to maximise multi-agency working between social work and substance use services?

Recommended resources

⮕ **Social work, alcohol and drugs:** www.swalcdrugs.com – a site for social workers offering information on many aspects of alcohol and drug use and interventions.

⮕ **Alcohol Concern:** www.alcoholconcern.org.uk – a website for the UK's leading national charity Alcohol Concern. It provides lots of useful information and facts as well as publications and an online directory of alcohol services.

⮕ **Adfam:** www.adfam.org.uk – a charitable organisation supporting families where there are concerns over alcohol or drug use. Publications and service links are available.

⮕ **Drugscope:** www.drugscope.org.uk – a website for the UK's leading national charity providing information on drugs, Drugscope. It provides factual advice, access to literature and a good reference library as well as a directory of drug agencies under its 'Helpfinder' facility.

⮕ **The National Treatment Agency:** www.nta.nhs.uk. Policy documents and practice guidance are available as well as details of the NTA's work programme and research briefing. Also contains a residential services directory.

> ➲ **Talk to Frank:** www.talktofrank.com – a government-funded website primarily designed for young people and anyone who wants to know more about specific drugs and their effects. Also has links to helplines.

References

Adams, P. (1999) 'Towards a family support approach with drug-using parents: the importance of social worker attitudes and knowledge', *Child Abuse Review*, vol 8, no 1, pp 15-28.

Adfam/Rethink (2004) *Living with Severe Mental Health and Substance Use Problems: Report from the Rethink Dual Diagnosis Research Group*, London: Rethink.

Advisory Council on the Misuse of Drugs (2003) *Hidden Harm: Responding to the Needs of Children of Problem Drug Users*, London: Home Office.

Altshuler, S.J. (2005) 'Drug-endangered children need a collaborative community response', *Child Welfare*, vol 84, no 2, pp 171-90.

Azrin, N.H. (1976) 'Improvements in the community-reinforcement approach to alcoholism', *Behavioural Research and Therapy*, vol 14, no 3, pp 339-48.

Barber, J. (2002) *Social Work with Addictions* (2nd edition), Basingstoke: Palgrave Macmillan.

Bear, Z., Griffiths, R. and Pearson, B. (2000) *Childhood Sexual Abuse and Substance Use*, London: The Centre for Research on Drugs and Health Behaviour.

BMA (British Medical Association) (2006) *Child and Adolescent Mental Health: A Guide for Health Care Professionals*, London: BMA.

Cabinet Office (2004) *The National Alcohol Harm Reduction Strategy*, London: Cabinet Office.

Cleaver, H., Nicholson, D., Tarr, S. and Cleaver, D. (2006) *The Response of Child Protection Practices and Procedures to Children Exposed to Domestic Violence or Parental Substance Misuse: Executive Summary*, www.dfes.gov.uk/research/data/uploadfiles/RW89%20r.pdf

Copello, A., Williamson, E., Orford, J. and Day, E. (2006) 'Implementing and evaluating Social Behaviour and Network Therapy in drug treatment practice in the UK: a feasibility study', *Addictive Behaviors*, vol 31, no 5, pp 802-10.

Corbin, W.R., Bernat, J.A., Calhoun, K.S., McNair, L.D. and Seals, K.L. (2001) 'The role of alcohol expectancies and alcohol consumption among sexually victimized and nonvictimized college women', *Journal of Interpersonal Violence*, vol 16, no 4, pp 297-311.

Costello, R.M. (1980) 'Alcoholism treatment effectiveness: slicing the outcome variance pie', in G. Edwards and M. Grant (eds) *Alcoholism Treatment in Transition*, London: Croom Helm.

DeWit, D.J., Adlaf, E.M., Offord, D.R. and Ogborne, A.C. (2000) 'Age at first alcohol use: a risk factor for the development of alcohol disorders', *American Journal of Psychiatry*, vol 157, no 5, pp 745–50.

DfES(Department for Education and Skills)/Home Office/DH (Department of Health) (2005) *Every Child Matters: Change for Children:Young People and Drugs*, London: DfES.

DH (2002) *Mental Health Policy Implementation Guide: Dual Diagnosis Good Practice Guide*, London: DH.

DH (2006) *Models of Care for the Treatment of Alcohol Misusers (MoCAM)*, London: NTA.

DH/HO (Home Office) (2006) *Models of Care for the Treatment of Adult Drug Misusers: Update 2006*, London: NTA.

Dillon, L., Chivite-Matthews, N., Grewal, I., Brown, R., Webster, S., Weddell, E., Brown, G. and Smith, N. (2007) *Risk, Protective Factors and Resilience to Drug Use: Identifying Resilient Young People and Learning from their Experiences*, Home Office Online Report 04/07, http://www.homeoffice.gov.uk/rds/pdfs07/rdsolr0407.pdf

Dobkin, P.L., De Civita, M., Paraherakis, A. and Gill, K. (2002) 'The role of functional social support in treatment retention and outcomes among outpatient adult substance abusers' *Addiction*, vol 97, no 3, pp 347–56.

Downs, W.R. and Harrison, L. (1998) 'Childhood maltreatment and the risk of substance problems in later life', *Health & Social Care in the Community*, vol 6, no 1, pp 35–46.

Downs, W.R., Miller, B.A. and Panek, D.E. (1993) 'Differential patterns of partner-to-woman violence: a comparison of samples of community, alcohol–abusing, and battered women', *Journal of Family Violence*, vol 8, no 2, pp 113–35.

Forrester, D. and Harwin, J. (2006) 'Parental substance misuse and child care social work: findings from the first stage of a study of 100 families', *Child and Family Social Work*, vol 11, pp 325–35.

Frisher, M., Crome, I., Macleod, J., Bloor, R. and Hickman, M. (2007) *Predictive Factors for Illicit Drug Use among Young People: A Literature Review*, Home Office Online Report 05/07, www.homeoffice.gov.uk/rds/pdfs07/rdsolr0507.pdf

Galvani, S. (2007) 'Refusing to listen: are we failing the needs of people with alcohol and drug problems?', *Social Work Education*, vol 26, no 7, pp 697–707.

Galvani, S. and Hughes, N. (in preparation) 'Working with alcohol and drug use: exploring the knowledge and attitudes of social work students'.

GSCC (General Social Care Council) (2005) *Specialist Standards and Requirements for Post-qualifying Programmes: Children and Young People, their Families and Carers*, London: GSCC.

Guy, P. and Harrison, L. (2003) 'Evidence-based social work with people who have substance problems', in J. Howarth and S.M. Shardlow (eds) *Making Links Across Specialisms*, Lyme Regis: Russell House Publishing.

Harman, K. and Paylor, I. (2005) 'An evaluation of the CARAT Initiative', *Howard Journal of Criminal Justice*, vol 44, no 4, pp 357-73.

Harrison, L. (ed) (1996) *Alcohol Problems in the Community*, London: Routledge.

Harwin, J. and Forrester, D. (2002) 'Parental substance misuse and child welfare: a study of social work with families in which parents misuse drugs or alcohol', First stage report for the Nuffield Foundation (unpublished).

Health Advisory Service (2000) *Commissioning Standards: Drug and Alcohol Treatment and Care*, London: The Substance Misuse Advisory Service.

Hogg, C. (1997) *Drug Using Parents: Policy Guidelines for Inter-agency Working*, London: DH.

Home Office (2002) *Updated Drugs Strategy 2002*, London: Home Office.

Jones, M., Kimberlee, R. and Powell, J. (2003) 'Commissioning drug services for vulnerable young people', *Drugs: Education, Prevention and Policy*, vol 10, no 3, pp 251-62.

Kearney, P., Levin, E. and Rosen, G. (2003a) *Alcohol, Drugs and Mental Health Problems: Working with Families*, London: Social Care Institute for Excellence.

Kearney, P., Levin, E., Rosen, G. and Sainsbury, M. (2003b) *Families that have Alcohol and Mental Health Problems: A Template for Partnership Working*, London: Social Care Institute for Excellence.

Kharicha, K., Levin, E., Iliffe, S. and Davey, B. (2004) 'Social work, general practice and evidence-based policy in the collaborative care of older people: current problems and future possibilities', *Health and Social Care in the Community*, vol 12, no 2, pp 134-41.

Lawson, A. (1994) 'Identification of and responses to problem drinking amongst social services users', *British Journal of Social Work*, vol 24, pp 325-42.

McCarthy, T. and Galvani, S. (2004) 'SCARS: a new model for social work with substance users', *Practice*, vol 16, no 2, pp 85-97.

Minkes, J., Hammersley, R. and Raynor, P. (2005) 'Partnership in working with young offenders with substance misuse problems', *The Howard Journal of Criminal Justice*, vol 44, no 3, pp 254-68.

NTA (National Treatment Agency) (2006) *Care Planning Practice Guide*, London: NTA.

Powell, B.J., Landon, J.F., Cantrell, P.J., Penick, E.C., Nickel, E.J., Liskow, B.I., Coddington, T.M., Campbell, J.L., Dale, T.M., Vance, M.D. and Rice, A.S. (1998) 'Prediction of drinking outcomes for male alcoholics after 10 to 14 years', *Alcoholism: Clinical and Experimental Research*, vol 22, no 3, pp 559-66.

Powell, J., Jones, M. and Kimberlee, R. (2003) 'Commissioning drug services for vulnerable young people', *Drugs: Education, Prevention and Policy*, vol 10, no 3, pp 251-62.

Rhodes, T., Lilly, R., Fernandez, C., Giorgino, E., Kemmesis, U.E., Ossebaard, H.C., Lalam, N., Faasen, I. and Spannow, K.E. (2003) 'Risk factors associated with drug use: the importance of "risk environment"', *Drugs: Education, Prevention and Policy*, vol 10, no 4, pp 303-29.

Sinclair, R. and Bullock, R. (2002) *Learning from Past Experience: A Review of Serious Case Reviews*, London: DH, www.dh.gov.uk/assetRoot/04/05/94/68/04059468.pdf

Stella Project (2004) *Domestic Violence, Drugs And Alcohol: Good Practice Guidelines*, London: The Stella Project.

Vanderplasschen, W., Rapp, R.C., Wolf, J. and Broekaert, E. (2006) 'Case management', *Drug and Alcohol Findings*, vol 15, pp 14-19.

Weaver, T. et al (2002) *Co-morbidity of Substance Misuse and Mental Illness Collaborative Study (COSMIC)*, London: DH/NTA.

Women's Aid (2005a) *Principles of Good Practice for Working with Women Who Use Substances*, www.womensaid.org.uk/landing_page.asp?section=0001 0001001000004000200020003, accessed 8 February 2007.

Women's Aid (2005b) *Principles of Good Practice for Working with Women Experiencing Domestic Violence: Guidance for Those Working in the Drug and Alcohol Sectors*, www.womensaid.org.uk/landing_page.asp?section=00010 0010010000400020002, accessed 8 February 2007.

Multi-agency working and partnership in services for adults with learning disabilities

Nicki Ward

Introduction

This chapter explores issues of multi-agency working in services for adults with learning disabilities. It considers the way that multi-agency working has featured in services for people with learning disabilities throughout the past 30 years, examines developments in services for people with learning disabilities and explores the implications of these developments for the social work role.

Throughout the chapter the term 'learning disability' is used to refer to those people who have:

> A significantly reduced ability to understand new or complex information, to learn new skills ... [and] ... a reduced ability to cope independently ... which started before adulthood and has a lasting effect on development. (DH, 2001, p 14)

BOX 8.1: *Glossary of terms used*	
LA	local authority
1990 NHSCCA	1990 National Health Service and Community Care Act
PCT	primary care trust

The learning disabled population

There are no accurate figures on the numbers of people with learning disabilities currently living in the UK. Estimates suggest between 985,000 and 1.4 million people (DH, 2001; Emerson et al, 2004), with this figure expected to increase by around 1% a year mainly due to improved healthcare and consequently increased life expectancy (DH, 2001). There are more men with learning disabilities than women, young people and people from South Asian communities are most likely to have severe learning disabilities, while mild learning disabilities are more common among young people and people who are poor or have other 'adverse' family backgrounds (Foundation for People with Learning Disabilities, 2003).

In 2003 it was estimated that around £4.6 billion was being spent on services for children and adults with learning disabilities; for adults the majority of this spending is on residential and day services (Foundation for People with Learning Disabilities, 2003). Adults with learning disabilities are more likely to be living with their parents or in residential accommodation and are far less likely to live independently or with a partner than the rest of the population. People with learning disabilities are more likely than the general population and the disabled population to be unemployed. Of the 800,000 adults with learning disabilities of working age, only 11% are estimated to have a job (Morgan and Beyer, 2005), and of those who are working most are working part time; one study found that 28% of men and 47% of women with learning disabilities who were in paid employment worked less than 16 hours a week (Emerson et al, 2004). People with learning disabilities are more likely to have experienced verbal abuse, while those with learning disabilities who are from black and minority ethnic groups are also likely to face racism (DH, 2001). In this context the government has recognised that the learning disabled population is among the most socially excluded in our society (DH, 2001).

Multi-agency working and services for people with learning disabilities: an ongoing relationship

The concept of multidisciplinary working in services for people with learning disabilities is not a new one. In 1977 the National Development Group for the Mentally Handicapped noted that 'staffing patterns and ... staff training programmes should increasingly reflect an interdisciplinary approach' (p 29). Thirty years ago, as a care assistant working in day centres with adults who had learning disabilities, I was conscious that the unit in which I worked was part of a 'multidisciplinary service'. The unit was funded and staffed by social services but also drew on the expertise of a variety of health professionals including physiotherapists, speech therapists, dentists and psychiatrists. This remained part of my experience; during the 1980s the area I worked in had a community learning disabilities team. This team combined health and social care professionals, primarily social workers and community nurses, who were co-located in a building geographically central to the area in the north of the city which they served. The White Paper *Valuing People: A New Strategy for Learning Disability for the 21st Century* (DH, 2001) notes that community learning disability teams were forerunners in partnership working but suggests that this has not been consolidated.

There are philosophical and practical differences between the initiatives of 20 or 30 years ago and the ones we see today. Philosophically there has been a shift from what was, primarily, a paternalistic, 'medical model' of services for adults with learning disabilities to one that can be perceived as more 'social', focused on rights, choice and self-advocacy. In this conception the professional is no longer the 'expert' but is a partner along with the person with the learning disability, their families, friends and supporters, and other professionals. Along with this philosophical shift there has been a change in service provision. In the 1970s and 1980s there was a move from long-term, segregated, institutional settings to more community-based services such as group homes or day services, and this was combined with a shift in responsibility for services from health authorities to local authorities, particularly social services. Since the 1990s there has been an increasing emphasis on independent living and the use of mainstream community services. This, along with changes in legislation and the promotion of a mixed economy of care, has meant that multi-agency working is no longer just about partnerships between health and social services. In the current climate those supporting people with learning disabilities are likely to include professionals working in a diverse range of statutory, voluntary and private sector services.

The legislative and policy framework

It has been suggested that for the New Labour government, 'modernisation' and those changes introduced under this agenda are 'shorthand' for public sector reform (Driver, 2005, p 265). The modernisation agenda has encompassed fundamental changes to the traditional social democratic position on the role of the state in the provision of public services. There have been two key aspects to this modernisation programme: first, an emphasis on 'consumers' that privileges the interests of service users rather than those of service providers, the 'producers' of services. Second, there was a decision that the government would take a 'pragmatic' approach to service delivery, which meant that delivery by the public sector was not automatically seen as either the best or the most financially appropriate model of service delivery (see, for example, Cabinet Office, 1999; Office for Public Services Reform, 2002). Partnership is a significant part of the modernisation agenda, and partnership working has become a central feature of many policy initiatives (Powell and Glendenning, 2002); this has emphasised the need for multi-agency working. This reflects an acknowledgement that social policy problems are multidimensional and can therefore only be addressed through multi–agency working. This is apparent in general health and social care policies (DH, 1998; the 1999 Health Act), as well as in those policies specifically designed to meet the needs of people with learning disabilities. As noted above, the notion of partnership and multidisciplinary working has been evident within legislative and policy framework for many years; however, recent developments have strengthened this position and put in place a number of strategies to facilitate working between agencies and across the traditional organisational boundaries. This section will outline the key aspects of policy and legislation that are pertinent to multi–agency working in services for people with learning disabilities (for a summary see Box 8.2).

- The 1990 National Health Service and Community Care Act (1990 NHSCCA) emphasised the need for joint planning and partnership working, especially between health and social services. However, at the same time it effectively created a greater division between health and social care by distinguishing between medical needs and social needs; any person who was deemed to have a medical as well as a social need became the responsibility of health services. This meant that day and residential services that came under the jurisdiction of the local authority social services department could no longer provide medical care, and in practice some day and residential services were compelled to withdraw the service from people who required emergency medical treatment. A further aspect of the 1990 NHSCCA that is pertinent to this discussion is the introduction of the 'purchaser–provider split' and the strategies that were introduced to encourage the development of a 'mixed economy of care'. These developments led to an increase in the number of domiciliary, day and residential services being provided by the voluntary and independent sector.
- *Modernising Social Services* (DH, 1998) identified that poor coordination between agencies was the reason for some aspects of poor service delivery. Here multi–agency working was seen as being broader than health and social care, with the emphasis being placed on service quality rather than on who provided service. One emphasis was on the inclusion of housing services.
- The 1999 Health Act made it possible for funding to be combined to enable greater joint working and in some cases integrated services and budgets. Section 31 of the Act permits agreements between local authorities (LAs) and primary care trusts (PCTs) and the setting up of care trusts that would have defined arrangements for partnership working, pooled budgets, lead commissioning responsibilities and integrated provisions. In this context, while the LA is accountable, the PCT may have responsibility to provide and commission the services. Section 31 of

the 1999 Health Act introduced 'flexibilities' designed to reduce barriers to working in partnership; these flexibilities were focused on three areas: pooled budgets, the delegation of commissioning responsibilities and integration of services or elements of services (1999 Health Act; Freeman and Peck, 2006).

- *Improving the Life Chances of Disabled People* (Cabinet Office, 2005) introduced individual budgets that were designed to combine resources from a range of different services, including health, housing and social services, as well as work resources from the Department for Work and Pensions and funds from the Independent Living Fund. This amount is then made 'transparent' to the individual, who uses the budget to purchase 'a flexible range of different types of support' (Glendinning and Means, 2006, p 17). This initiative was inspired by 'in Control', a partnership between the Valuing People support team, Mencap and Care Services Improvement Partnership (CSIP), and has been piloted by some LAs and a number of independent organisations in services for people with learning disabilities.

- The White Paper *Our Health, Our Care, Our Say: A New Direction for Community Services* (DH, 2006), and the Green Paper *Independence, Well-Being and Choice* (DH, 2005) that preceded it, set out the government's vision for social care services for the following 10-15 years. This vision included:

  - partnership and integrated services;
  - better use of technology and housing options;
  - individual budgets and better use of direct payments;
  - streamlined processes, to include joint assessments across agencies and professions such as health, social services, housing and benefits services.

Encapsulated within this legislation is an indication of just how diverse multi-agency working needs to become if effective services are to be developed.

- In relation to services for people with learning disabilities, the primary piece of legislation, which provides a framework for all learning disability services, is *Valuing People* (DH, 2001), within which partnership working is seen as central: 'effective partnership working by all agencies is the key to achieving social inclusion for people with learning disabilities' (DH, 2001, p 8). *Valuing People* embraced the principles of advocacy and self-determination and put forward four key principles for learning disability services – rights, independence, choice and inclusion – arguing that people with learning disabilities should have far greater access to community services and greater choice and control over how and where they should live.

BOX 8.2: *Summary: the legislative framework*

Title	Emphasis and key initiatives
1990 NHSCCA	Joint planning and partnership between health and social care. Introduction and promotion of the 'mixed economy of care'.
Modernising Social Services (DH, 1998)	Identified need for greater coordination between services and introduced a broader conception of 'multi-agency working'.
1999 Health Act	Emphasised joint working and integrated services, made provision for creation of care trusts and 'flexibilities' to aid this.
Improving the Life Chances of Disabled People (Cabinet Office, 2005)	Individual budgets to combine resources from a range of service providers and provide greater control to service users.
Our Health, Our Care, Our Say (DH, 2006)	Partnership and integrated services, streamlined assessments and greater use of individual budgets.
Valuing People (DH, 2001)	Partnership working as 'key' to social inclusion for people with learning disabilities. Four key principles: rights, independence, choice and inclusion.

In recent years the legislative framework has increased the possibilities for partnership working between services while also introducing new opportunities to work in ways that give people with learning disabilities increased control over the services they receive. This reflects recognition that, while people with learning disabilities have increasingly been living within local communities, they have continued to face barriers in using ordinary community facilities and services. For this situation to improve there is a need for the agencies involved in multi-agency working to become increasingly diverse. The area of adult protection is one which clearly illustrates the increasing diversity and complexity of multi-agency partnerships (see Box 8.3).

BOX 8.3: *Partners in adult protection*

The document *Safeguarding Adults*, published by the Association of Directors of Social Services (ADSS, 2005), contains a table that demonstrates the 'partners' who should be involved in safeguarding adults. In relation to people with learning disabilities this might include:

Statutory organisations	Other potential members	Links to other partnerships
LA • Adult social services • Housing • Welfare rights/ benefits • Education/ community • Education • Legal services • Licensing Police Crown Prosecution Service Probation PCTs Other NHS care trusts Hospital trusts Commission for Social Care Inspection Healthcare Commission Strategic health authority Housing trusts Supporting People Board Department for Work and Pensions	Service users'/patients' organisations Carers' organisations Advocacy providers Direct payments 'Umbrella' organisations Care home and domiciliary care providers/ associations Supporting People providers Victim support services, eg Victim Support, Rape Crisis, Women's Aid, VOICE UK, Respond Voluntary sector service providers, eg People First, MENCAP Voluntary sector groups working against abuse of adults, eg Ann Craft Trust, PAVA, WITNESS	Local Strategic Partnerships • Regeneration • Health • Crime and Disorder Reduction Board • Domestic violence • Drugs and alcohol • Neighbourhood forums/ communities of interest MAPPA (Multi-Agency Public Protection Arrangements) Joint planning and commissioning for people with learning disabilities Carers

Source: Adapted from ADSS (2005)

The ability of social workers, as advocates and care managers, to respond to the individual needs of people with learning disabilities necessitates an increase in the diversity of services available. However, research on services for people with learning disabilities continues to highlight the lack of choice that people have. Greater choice is needed in relation to living accommodation, day services and respite care (Fruin, 1998), with many people still having no control over where to live and who should support them (Learning Disabilities Task Force, 2004). As the discussion earlier illustrated, many people with learning disabilities continue to live with their parents, and when parents are no longer able to support them they move to residential care. Few people are offered the opportunity to live independently in their own home or supported to stay in the family home. Improved domiciliary services that were better able to understand the needs of people with learning disabilities would increase opportunities for independent living (Fruin, 1998; Learning Disabilities Task Force, 2004). Meeting the core values of rights, independence, choice and inclusion has implications for multi-agency working which reach beyond the traditional health and social care partnerships. If people with learning disabilities are to be fully included in their local communities, this will involve greater use of leisure facilities and improved access to transport. Giving people with learning disabilities more choice over where to live will require more creative use of housing services, while enabling greater independence and opportunities for financial inclusion will require the skills and knowledge of those working in further and higher education and employment services. In addition, partnerships with health providers need to move beyond partnerships between specialist segregated services. People with learning disabilities often have greater primary healthcare needs than the general population but these needs are also more likely to go unmet (Lennox et al, 2003), and this suggests that multi-agency working needs to incorporate partnerships between people with learning disabilities, support workers, general pracitioners, dentists, chiropodists and district nurses in order to improve access to healthcare. The following section identifies some of the potential difficulties that workers might face in working collaboratively within a multi-agency setting.

The problems of partnership – lessons from research and practice

As illustrated earlier, the legislative and policy framework for social care generally, and for people with learning disabilities more specifically, has increasingly emphasised the need for multi-agency working and, at a strategic level at least, frameworks have been put in place to encourage this. However, despite the developments implemented since 2001, many services are still not working well together (Cope, 2003). The Learning Disabilities Task Force (2004, p 16) found that 'Services like health, social services and education do not always work together to support people; sometimes people get services that are not right for them'.

Effective multi-agency working requires change at organisational, agency and individual level and can often present a challenge to professional cultures (Sloper, 2004). Some of the barriers to partnership may be structural or institutional, such as the distinctions made between medical and social needs in determining care, for example, and government policy has aimed to remove some of these barriers. However, many of the barriers can be conceptualised as ideological boundaries. One example of this might be distinctions between the social model values favoured by social workers and the medical model that we, as social workers, often assume is the dominating ideology among health professionals. There is evidence that social workers may have anxieties about the diminishing of a social model perspective and that health perspectives mean a dominance of the medical model (Abbott et al, 2005). This is an issue that has been reflected to me by students on placement in areas that have traditionally been the domain of health professionals.

Hudson et al (2002), in an evaluation of section 31 initiatives (see discussion on pp 130–31), found that a number of things were important for their success, including trust and leadership, local commitment and the promotion of holistic professional working practices. They argued that while the strategies put in place at a national level would encourage new initiatives, for these to succeed required agency and local organisation commitment. Structural changes that provide a policy framework for partnership are important, but on their own they are unlikely to deliver change (Hudson et al, 2002; SSI and Audit Commission, 2003).

Some aspects of the new legislative framework suggest that roles may become less clearly defined, with community nurses as well as social workers having care management responsibilities, for example, and these can be difficult circumstances to negotiate. The adaptation of what are traditional roles can present both opportunities and threats (Brown et al, 2000): on one level it may present opportunities for staff to take on new and different roles and to be free from organisational and structural confines, but at the same time workers may feel that their own expertise is being undervalued. The case study in Practice Example 1 illustrates the issues raised:

Practice Example 1

Case study – Rosa

Rosa is 60 years old; she lives with her sister Moira who is 75. Rosa attends the local day centre where she has been going for many years.

Ellie is a community day services coordinator who has worked with people with learning disabilities for 12 years and for the past four years she has been working with Rosa. Lena is a community nurse who has recently joined the team; she has begun working with Rosa and Moira, exploring possibilities for Rosa to live independently.

Ellie has arranged a holiday for three of the people that she works with, including Rosa whom she has been working with for three years. Rosa has to take insulin via an injection twice a day. As Ellie has previously been away with Rosa, she has received training so that she can help Rosa with her medication. This training was updated two weeks ago. Lena approaches Ellie at the day centre to inform her that she is arranging a review meeting. In the course of the discussion Ellie tells Lena that one of the proposed dates will not be acceptable as it is the week of the holiday. Lena asks who will be supporting Rosa with her medication and when Ellie says that she will, Lena expresses concern that Ellie is not medically qualified to do this.

In this situation both Lena and Ellie were left feeling that they had had their particular areas of expertise undermined. The two did not know each other well and Ellie was already upset that Lena, who she felt did not know Rosa and her sister as well as she did, had been appointed to work with the family during this important transition in their lives. Lena was threatened by the relationship that Ellie apparently had with the family, and it seemed that each time she visited Moira and Rosa they talked about Ellie. She was genuinely concerned about safety issues, as well as feeling that this was one area where her own expertise might be of value.

This case study illustrates the way that individual workers may become wary of each other and may feel their own particular knowledge and expertise is being undervalued. To practise effectively in a multidisciplinary context social workers need to be clear about both their own roles and responsibilities and those of others.

As services change and develop, workers are likely to have concerns about their own roles and professional identity. It is important that people are clear about their particular expertise and that they do not feel that this is being threatened or demeaned. For partnerships to be effective people need to be honest with each other and have space to develop trusting relationships based on shared understanding and values (Lofthouse et al, 2002; SSI and Audit Commission, 2003). One of the barriers to effective partnership working is a lack of space to develop relationships. Research by Hudson et al (1997) found that collaboration is most effective when there are opportunities to develop trusting and respectful local networks rather than when conditions are imposed on teams. People cannot be expected to work together without an understanding of each other's specialist expertise and space to develop common goals (Robinson and Cottrell, 2005). While multi-agency working presents a challenge to social workers it also represents a positive opportunity for creativity and personal development. Abbott et al (2005), in research conducted with different professionals involved in multi-agency working, found that those interviewed enjoyed working in a multi-agency context and that it provided opportunities for staff to develop new knowledge and skills. One of the most valued aspects of knowledge was understanding the roles and responsibilities of others. Having such an understanding can increase trust and therefore facilitate greater collaborative working:

> 'I used to work for a voluntary agency and we all thought social workers were terrible as you couldn't get hold of them and they never returned your calls. Then I went to work for social services and I realised that it wasn't that they didn't want to talk to you, they just didn't have the time.'

This quote from a student social worker reinforces the findings of Abbott et al (2005), which suggests that one positive benefit of multi-agency working is the erosion of 'blame culture' as a result of having a greater understanding of the roles and responsibilities of other people.

Structural changes are only effective when there are efforts to develop shared values and a common culture, which includes clarity and shared purpose (SSI and Audit Commission, 2003). Language and communication can be a barrier to effective partnership and multi-agency working both for adults with learning disabilities and for the different professionals involved:

> 'Professionals need to remember that they have spent years learning their jobs and the language that goes with it. To people with learning difficulties, listening to jargon in meetings can be like trying to understand a different language'. (Brian White, Co-chair of the National Forum for People with Learning Difficulties, cited in Lofthouse et al, 2002, p 11)

The experience of people with learning difficulties from marginalised communities is further impacted by the barriers of discrimination and oppression.

This use of jargon and professional language can also impact upon interprofessional relationships. The same person may be referred to differently, as a client, a carer, a patient, a service user, a customer, a tenant or a resident, for example, and this can translate into different conceptualisations of a person and their needs. White and Featherstone (2005) illustrate the difficulty of developing partnerships and using shared tools such as a Common Assessment Framework within this context, noting that even where different professionals are co-located there can still be difficulties with professional language and cultures. Some of these issues are reflected in the case study presented in Practice Example 2.

Practice Example 2

Case study – Arnold

Arnold Laker lives independently in a council flat. The flat used to be his mother's but when she died three years ago Arnold was granted right of succession and the tenancy passed to him. At this time the local housing officer, Mohammed, liaised with the neighbourhood office, which assisted Arnold with a claim for Housing Benefit and Council Tax Benefit. At the same time Mohammed also made a referral to social services to ask for an assessment to be done as he felt that Arnold may need some support.

Arnold's mother, Mrs Laker, was a very thrifty woman; having lived through the war and rationing, she had developed lots of strategies for saving money and recycling. She kept her newspapers for lighting the fire and butter wrappers to grease the trays when baking, while jars were kept for pickling. Mrs Laker had been a seamstress so she always kept the buttons and fasteners off old clothes. Since her death, Arnold has continued to save these materials. Social services have recently received a complaint from Arnold's neighbours that the property is unsanitary. A social worker, Mary, visits but Arnold will not answer the door. Mrs Laker had always warned Arnold not to let strangers in. After numerous attempts Mary eventually 'catches' Arnold in the hall and is able to secure an invite into his flat. In her case notes Mary describes having to step over piles of newspapers and the smell from the heaps of butter wrappers and unwashed milk cartons that are kept around the kitchen. Her notes suggest that the flat is 'unsanitary and unsafe' and she expresses concern that the property has no central heating and that Arnold sits very close to the gas fire, which is surrounded by newspapers. Arnold says he leaves the fire on 24 hours a day and he sleeps in his armchair next to the fire. When she returns to the office she sends a fax to the housing department, which is located in the office upstairs, saying that they need to arrange for central heating to be installed, for environmental services to clean the property and for the floor coverings to be replaced throughout the property.

As this case study illustrates, effective practice in an interdisciplinary setting means seeing beyond traditional alliances and partnerships; on a practical level this means that social workers must be prepared to forge relationships with a wide range of public and private service providers and be committed to developing an awareness of the structures that guide the work of these new partners.

Towards best practice

Coulshed and Orme (2006, p 50) note that liaison and negotiation skills are 'paramount' for effective partnership working. This includes the need to recognise the expertise, status and concerns of all those who are involved. If the core values of *Valuing People* (DH, 2001) – rights, independence, choice and inclusion – are to be achieved then the first step in partnership working in services for people with learning disabilities needs to be to recognise the expertise they have about their own situation, their needs and their desires. In order to do this, professionals need to 'put aside' their professional cultures and language and learn to communicate in ways that are accessible to everyone. Being clear about the boundaries of your role, honest about the purpose of your involvement, not using jargon and not consulting other professionals or passing on information without the service user's permission are all important (Beckett and Maynard, 2005, p 165) and will help to create partnerships with service users. Locating these skills within an understanding of the history and traditions that different families and communities share is important in ensuring the accessibility of the service and the professional approach. For people with learning disabilities one important aspect of the social worker's role is to be able to translate the complex world of a mixed economy of care into a language that people with learning disabilities can understand (Concannon, 2006).

While evidence suggests that having structural and organisational frameworks to support multi–agency and interprofessional working is important, there are steps that social workers can take to enable them to make a difference to the individual lives of service users and their families and to experiences of multi-agency working. Elaine Monk, whose daughter Rachel has a learning disability, suggests that 'it all depends on the person really, I found that a lot over the years' (2005, p 212). Having greater control over the services received has been shown to impact on the lives of people with learning disabilities in positive ways and this is most often related to being enabled to use ordinary community services (in Control, 2006). Building a portfolio of accessible information and developing connections with colleagues in mainstream services will place social workers in a better position to enable people with learning disabilities to access flexible services.

Partnerships between different providers work best when those involved have a sense of shared purpose expressed in terms of outcomes for the service user and where 'there are wins for each partner' (SSI and Audit Commission, 2003). Working on ways to move forward together will be far more successful than making demands. It is important to find ways of engaging with people with learning disabilities and other stakeholders in ways that make sense to them (DH, 2002).

While it is important to maintain and develop partnerships between those more traditionally thought of as key stakeholders in services for people with learning disabilities, particularly health and social care, it is also important to broaden the service horizons. Knowledge of services and access to this knowledge needs to be improved. A survey of people with learning difficulties found that they were more likely to turn to support workers or family and friends for advice on housing, education and employment rather than the housing department, job centre or colleges, for example. Only 15% said they would turn to the careers service for advice, despite a majority noting that they would like to secure employment (Health and Social Care Information Centre, 2004). A report from the Department for Work and Pensions (Beyer et al, 2004) suggests that day services for people with learning disabilities need to develop stronger links with specialist employment agencies. However, work by the Foundation for People with Learning Disabilities (2003) suggests that many of the schemes in place to support disabled people in accessing employment are not sufficiently sensitive to the needs of people with learning disabilities and that they need to develop greater expertise in working with people with learning disabilities. Here social workers have a dual role – to develop awareness of these schemes and an understanding of what the employment agencies can provide, while also being able to provide information to assist these services in working with people with learning disabilities.

There is a need for greater flexibility in funding and the use of funds in order to create the spaces in which people with learning disabilities can exercise choice and independence. Results from in Control's first phase of using individual budgets found that there had been an increase in the use of personal assistants and a reduction in the use of traditional day centres (in Control, 2006). Social workers have a responsibility to ensure they are familiar with these options and are able to facilitate access to direct payments and individual budgets in order to promote service user control and self-determination.

Conclusion

Services for people with learning disabilities have a long history of multi-agency working, particularly between health and social care agencies. In the future there will be an increasingly complex web of individuals and organisations who need to work together with people with learning disabilities if the socially inclusive vision of *Valuing People* is to be achieved (DH, 2001, p 16), presenting both challenges and opportunities. Where people have been enabled to access mainstream community services they report increased satisfaction with services (in Control, 2006), and professionals involved in multi-agency teams also report positive experiences (Abbott et al, 2005). Nevertheless, research suggests that a general lack of trust and misunderstandings were the basis of problems in many partnerships (Audit Commission and SSI, 2004).

Recent policy developments have removed some of the structural barriers to partnership working, and people with learning disabilities are increasingly involved, along with professionals from statutory and voluntary agencies, in service development. User-based partnerships with councils are more prevalent than they were 10 years ago, and within adult services there has been an increase in partnership working in both the commissioning and provision of care (Audit Commission and SSI, 2004). The result of these policy developments is that there is now a body of evidence and guidance on good practice for working in partnership that has been developed in conjunction with people with learning disabilities. Lofthouse et al (2002), for example, provide the following checklist for thinking about whether partnerships will be effective:

- Do you all believe in the same thing?
- Do you all agree about what needs to change first?
- Are you all happy to look at new ways of doing things?
- Are you all clear about what we can and cannot do?
- Have you agreed who is going to do what?
- Does everybody understand what each organisation has agreed to give to the work (like money, staff or time)?

- Have you got good leaders?
- Are there people who can do the work, and have enough time?
- Do people trust each other and are people being honest with each other?

If organisations and service providers capitalise on this work, then services for people with learning disabilities may continue to be at the forefront of developments in multi-agency working.

Trigger questions

⮑ What are the challenges facing the development of multi-agency working in services for people with learning disabilities?

⮑ How might those using the services influence the development of multi-agency working?

⮑ What possibilities and opportunities does multi-agency working in this setting present?

Recommended resources

⮑ **Department of Health** (2002) *Keys to Partnership: Working Together to Make a Difference in People's Lives*, London: DH, www.integratedcarenetwork.gov.uk

⮑ **British Institute of Learning Disabilities**, www.bild.org.uk/

⮑ **Foundation for People with Learning Disabilities**, www.learningdisabilities.org.uk/

⮑ **Learning Disabilities Task Force**, www.dh.gov.uk/ en/Policyandguidance/Healthandsocialcaretopics/ Learningdisabilities/Learningdisabilitiestaskforce/index.htm

⮑ **in Control**, www.in-control.org.uk/

⮑ **Care Services Improvement Partnership**, www.csip.org.uk/

⮑ **Valuing People**, http://valuingpeople.gov.uk/index.jsp

References

Abbott, D., Townsley, R. and Watson, D. (2005) 'Multi–agency working in services for disabled children: what impact does it have on professionals?', *Health and Social Care in the Community*, vol 13, no 2, pp 155-63.

ADSS (Association for Directors of Social Services) (2005) *Safeguarding Adults: A National Framework of Standards for Good Practice and Outcomes in Adult Protection Work*, London: ADSS.

Audit Commission and SSI (Social Services Inspectorate) (2004) *Old Virtues, New Virtues: An Overview of the Changes in Social Care Services over the Seven Years of the Joint Reviews in England 1996–2003*, London: Audit Commission.

Beckett, C. and Maynard, A. (2005) *Values and Ethics in Social Work: An Introduction*, London: Sage Publications.

Beyer, S., Grove, R., Schneider, J., Simons, K., Williams, V., Heyman, A., Swift, P. and Krijnen-Kemp, E. (2004) *Working Lives: The Role of Day Centres in Supporting People with Learning Disabilities into Employment*, London: Department for Work and Pensions.

Brown, B., Crawford, P. and Darongkamas, J. (2000) 'Blurred roles and permeable boundaries: the experience of multidisciplinary working in community mental health', *Health and Social Care in the Community*, vol 8, no 6, pp 425-35.

Cabinet Office (1999) *Modernising Government*, Cm 4310, London: The Stationery Office.

Cabinet Office (2005) *Improving the Life Chances of Disabled People*, London: Cabinet Office Strategy Unit.

Concannon, L. (2006) 'Inclusion or control: commissioning and contracting services for people with learning disabilities', *British Journal of Learning Disabilities*, vol 34, pp 200-5.

Cope, C. (2003) *Fulfilling Lives: Inspection of Social Care Services for People with Learning Difficulties*, London: Department of Health and Social Services Inspectorate.

Coulshed, V. and Orme, J. (2006) *Social Work Practice* (4th edition), Basingstoke: Macmillan.

DH (Department of Health) (1998) *Modernising Social Services*, London: HMSO.

DH (2001) *Valuing People: A New Strategy for Learning Disability for the 21st Century*, London: HMSO.

DH (2002) *Keys to Partnership: Working Together to Make a Difference in People's Lives*, London: DH.

DH (2005) *Independence, Well-being and Choice*, London: HMSO.

DH (2006) *Our Health, Our Care, Our Say*, London: HMSO.

Driver, S. (2005) 'Welfare after Thatcherism: New Labour and social democratic politics', in M. Powell, L. Bauld and K. Clarke (2005) *Social Policy Review 17*, Bristol: The Policy Press.

Emerson, E., Malam, S., Davies, I. and Spencer, K. (2004) *Adults with Learning Difficulties in England 2003/04*, London: National Statistics and NHS Health and Social Care Information Centre.

Foundation for People with Learning Disabilities (2003) Statistics on Learning Disability, London: Foundation for People with Learning Disabilities, www.learningdisabilities.org.uk/page.cfm?pagecode=ISBISTBI

Freeman, T. and Peck, E. (2006) 'Evaluating partnerships: a case study of integrated specialist mental health services', *Health and Social Care in the Community*, vol 14, no 5, pp 408-17.

Fruin, D. (1998) *Moving into the Mainstream: A Report of a National Inspection of Services for Adults with Learning Disabilities*, London: Department of Health and Social Services Inspectorate.

Glendinning, C. and Means, R. (2006) 'Personal social services: developments in adult social care', in L. Bauld, K. Clarke and T. Maltby (2006) *Social Policy Review 18*, Bristol: The Policy Press.

Health and Social Care Information Centre (2004) *Adults with Learning Difficulties in England 2003/04*, London: Office for National Statistics.

Hudson, B., Hardy, B., Henwood, M. and Wistow, G. (1997) 'Working across professional boundaries: primary health care and social care', *Public Money and Management*, vol 17, no 4, pp 25-30.

Hudson, B., Young, R., Hardy, B. and Glendinning, C. (2002) *National Evaluation of Notifications for Use of the Section 31 Partnership Flexibilities of the Health Act 1999*, Manchester: National Primary Care Research and Development Centre.

in Control (2006) *A Report on in Control's First Phase 2003–2005*, London: in Control Publications.

Learning Disabilities Task Force (2004) *Rights, Independence, Choice and Inclusion*, London: Learning Disabilities Taskforce.

Lennox, T., Nadkarna, J., Moffat, P. and Robertson, C. (2003) 'Access to services and meeting the needs of people with learning disabilities', *British Journal of Learning disabilities*, vol 7, pp 34-50.

Lofthouse, D., Barnes, L. and Mendonca, P. (2002) *Working Together: What Keys to Partnership is About*, London: DH.

Monk, E. (2005) 'Enriched lives', in S. Rolph, D. Atkinson, M. Mind and J. Welshman (eds) *Witness to Change: Families, Learning Difficulties and History*, Kidderminster: BILD.

Morgan, H. and Beyer, S. (2005) *Employment and People with Learning Disabilities: A Policy Briefing*, London: Foundation for People with Learning Disabilities.

National Development Group for the Mentally Handicapped (1977) *Pamphlet 5: Day Services for Mentally Handicapped Adults*, London: NDGMG.

Office for Public Services Reform (2002) *Reforming our Public Services*, London: Cabinet Office.

Powell, M. and Glendinning, C. (2002) 'Introduction', in C. Glendinning, M. Powell and K. Rummery (eds) *Partnerships, New Labour and the Governance of Welfare*, Bristol: The Policy Press, pp 1-14.

Robinson, M. and Cottrell, D. (2005) 'Health professionals in multi-disciplinary and multi-agency teams: changing professional practice', *Journal of Interprofessional Care*, vol 19, no 6, pp 547-60.

Sloper, P. (2004) 'Facilitators and barriers for co-coordinated multi-agency services', *Child Care, Health and Development*, vol 30, no 6, pp 571-80.

SSI (Social Services Inspectorate) and Audit Commission (2003) *Old Virtues, New Virtues: Seven Years of Joint Reviews in England 1996–2003*, Leeds: Audit Commission.

White, S. and Featherstone, B. (2005) 'Communicating misunderstandings: multi-agency work as social practice', *Child and Family Social Work*, vol 10, pp 207-16.

Social work practice with older people: working in partnership

Rosemary Littlechild

Introduction

'It seemed like quite a few people had pieces of the jigsaw but no one had the picture on the box.'

This remark from an older person (quoted in Hudson, 2006, p 5) illustrates that, generally, what older people are interested in is whether services join up and do what they need them to do, in the right way, at the right time. For them, professional boundaries, administrative wrangles and organisational disputes, which often accompany partnership working between professionals, are irrelevant (Glasby and Littlechild, 2004).

From the perspectives of service providers, social work professionals and older people themselves, partnership working is an important factor in the provision of care services for older people in the future. Joint working between health and social care professionals is particularly important for delivering services to older people as they are major consumers of health and social care services and often have complex health and social needs requiring responses from several services (Glasby and Littlechild, 2004).

The New Labour government has put partnership working and 'joined-up' service provision at the forefront of its social care and health policies for the 21st century (see, for example, DH, 2006a; ODPM, 2006) and social workers are increasingly working alongside colleagues from a variety of backgrounds, based in a range of public, voluntary and independent agencies. Social workers are therefore often in a good position to ensure that good partnership working improves the quality of services to older people and their experiences of those services. This chapter takes as its focus the way in which social workers can develop their working practices with other professionals and with older people themselves in order to achieve these two aims.

It examines what we mean by partnership working and how it fits within the context of current social work education and the changing legislative and policy framework, how partnership is working in practice, using evidence from research, and concludes with narratives from two social workers, identifying some practice learning points for effective partnership working.

BOX 9.1: *Glossary of terms used*	
GP	general practitioner
GSCC	General Social Care Council
POPPS	Partnership for Older People Projects

What do we mean by partnership working?

There is a wide range of terms used to explain the practice of different professionals from different agencies working together, described by Whittington (2003, p 16) as the 'lexicon of partnership and collaboration'. However, more important than commonality around definition is the emergence of some key features of a way of working, identified by Glasby and Littlechild (2004, p 7) as:

- a desire to achieve benefits that could not be attained by single agency working by itself;
- a recognition that some services are interdependent and that action in one part of the system will have a 'knock-on effect' somewhere else;
- some sort of shared vision of the way forward or shared purpose.

In order for this vision of partnership working to be effectively achieved, preparation must take place on a number of levels:

- strategic level – where agencies, often driven by government imperatives, plan and develop services together in order to use their resources more effectively;
- organisational level – where there is a focus on how different staff from different agencies can work together more effectively;
- practice level – where individual workers must examine their own practice, not only with their professional colleagues but with older people themselves and with those people who support them.

In relation to partnership working in services for older people, the focus has to date been largely on the strategic and organisational level and how well services are working together. As yet, there is little evidence about how partnership working improves the outcomes for older people and their carers (SCIE, 2006). In the current enthusiasm for collaborative working we must ensure that partnerships are a 'means to an end (that is, as a means to better services, experiences and outcomes for service users and carers)' and not an end in themselves (Glasby and Littlechild, 2004, p 3).

Partnership working in the context of social work education and social work with older people

Learning to work effectively with other professionals and with service users and carers is a key component of professional social work education and is a skill that all social workers must continue to develop in their ongoing professional development. The National Occupational Standards for Social Work (TOPPS, 2002, Key Role 5), the academic benchmarks for social work education (QAA, 2000, paras 3.12 and 3.1.5) and Codes of Practice from the General Social Care Council (GSCC, 2002, Section 6.7) all relate to collaborative social work practice and understanding inter-agency partnerships.

As standards have been established within social work education, social work has consolidated itself as a profession with further regulation by the General Social Care Council (GSCC), with which all qualified social workers must now be registered (Cree and Davis, 2007). However, a parallel development has been the restructuring of social services in England in 2005, which has led to the creation of separate services for children and families and for adults, leading potentially to the fragmentation of social work services (Cree and Davis, 2007).

Commentators (Postle, 2002; Lymbery, 2006) have argued that the community care reforms, in particular care management, have reduced the role of social workers and led to the rise of an administrative approach to social work with older people, 'which makes it hard to assert that practice with older people is more than simply a treadmill of routinised assessments leading to unimaginative packages of care' (Lymbery, 2006, p 1129). The role of qualified social workers within multidisciplinary teams for older people is therefore by no means assured.

Legislative and policy framework

The difficulties that currently beset health, social care and other welfare agencies in providing coordinated public services that meet the needs of older people are not new and have been well documented (see, for example, Means et al, 2002; Glasby and Littlechild, 2004; Parrott, 2006). Poor coordination, a lack of collaborative working and little accountability between agencies have been consistently cited as key factors contributing to the problem of the failure of the government to provide effective community care services (Audit Commission, 1986). In the community care reforms of the 1990s, the Conservative government reluctantly gave local authorities prime responsibility for coordinating community care services. However, as Parrott (2006, p 23) points out, 'Partnership at this time was less important than the further encouragement of alternative provision through the private and voluntary sectors', so that, ironically, the reforms designed to *promote* collaborative working between agencies actually brought about further fragmentation. Since the election of the New Labour government in 1997, there has been a plethora of legislation, policy and guidance designed to promote 'a new spirit of flexible partnership working' (DH, 1998). Recent policy documents have shifted to emphasise the importance of a 'systems approach' (Audit Commission, 2002; Hudson, 2006) and the need to appreciate the interdependency of a range of different services in meeting people's needs. In relation to older people, there is a new policy direction based on independence and choice and the commissioning of services with a greater focus on prevention and earlier intervention. Key policy documents are summarised in Box 9.2.

BOX 9.2: *Summary of key policy documents*

- *The 1999 Health Act* – introduced 'flexibilities', which lifted structural and administrative barriers between health and social services and enabled them to pool budgets, delegate commissioning and integrate services (see Glendinning et al, 2002).
- *The NHS Plan* (DH, 2000) – included the development of intermediate care services; a single assessment process for health and social care (both later developed in the National Service Framework for Older People [DH, 2001]); and the creation of new care trusts to deliver and commission health and social care services, a model formally introduced in the 2001 Health and Social Care Act (see Glasby and Peck, 2003).
- The White Paper *Our Health, Our Care, Our Say* (DH, 2006a) – included plans for a set of joint outcomes for use by health and social care professionals, the use of personal health and social care plans and a joint commissioning framework.
- *Investment in Partnership for Older People Projects (POPPS)* (DH, 2006b) – initiatives funded by government to show how innovative partnership arrangements between local authorities, primary care trusts (PCTs) and older people can lead to improved outcomes for older people.

- A consultative document *Opportunity Age: Meeting the Challenges of Ageing in the 21st Century* (HM Government, 2005) – a cross-government strategy advocating a more integrated approach to financial and benefit advice for older people.
- *A Sure Start to Later Life* (ODPM, 2006) – outlining how, using the same methods as the children's model to improve access, services can be brought together around older people and help reduce their social exclusion and improve their participation.

This chapter now looks at the evidence of how the rhetoric of partnership working is operating in practice.

Research evidence

Many of the initiatives identified above are in the early stages of implementation and have yet to be formally evaluated. Initial evidence from the projects is encouraging but is still at the descriptive stage. A review of the 19 projects funded by the Partnership for Older People Projects (POPPS) programme shows that many have developed a 'whole systems' approach to service design and delivery involving many different agencies and approaches (DH, 2006b). For example, a POPPS project in Somerset has set up 50 local Active Age Centres, based in existing local facilities (ODPM, 2006, p 33). Services include identification of older people at risk of falling, adult learning and leisure services with internet facilities, crime reduction initiatives and access to volunteering.

While there is a growing body of published literature about partnership working at a strategic and organisational level and in relation to interprofessional working, there is little evidence yet about the effects of partnership working on the lives of older people and their carers. This was the conclusion of Dowling et al (2004) in their literature review of research evidence published from 1997 onwards on the 'success' of partnerships in the health and social care fields. The authors conceptualised the success of partnerships in two main ways – as 'process' issues, focusing on how well services/partner agencies work together, and 'outcome' issues, such as whether the changes in services make an improvement to the lives of service users and carers.

Dowling et al (2004) found that the overwhelming majority of studies (31 out of 36) made a judgement about the success of partnerships on process criteria alone and in only five studies were outcome factors considered. In addition the authors found a dearth of evidence about the complex issues of the cost-effectiveness of partnerships and the difficulties of attributing success to the partnership itself rather than other factors.

Other examples of key research studies that have examined some aspects of partnership working include the following.

Partnership at strategic/organisational level

Glendinning et al (2002), evaluating the use of the 1999 Health Act flexibilities by local authorities and the NHS, found that removing structural, organisational and financial barriers, and in particular the pooling of funding streams, widened the vision for the planning and delivery of services and did assist the process of partnership working between agencies. However, this relaxing of boundaries alone was insufficient to produce effective partnership working, and additional internal barriers needed to be addressed, including difficulties over professional identities and differential power relations between newly integrated team members and other professionals.

Challis et al (2006) explored the question of whether integrated structures of health and social services impacted upon the operation of care management for older people, by comparing Trusts in Northern Ireland (where the delivery of health and social care is provided by one organisation) and local authorities in England. Despite certain methodological limitations in the study, they tentatively conclude that more integrated working practices were evident in Northern Ireland. Of particular interest was the use of more professionally qualified staff in the assessment and care management process in the integrated structure and the greater involvement of healthcare staff in assessment.

Interprofessional working

Hudson (2002) claims that too much attention has been focused on promoting partnership at an organisational level on the assumption that if more integrated structures are in place, more joined-up working practices will follow. On the contrary, he identifies that partnership working often fails because of disputes between professions based on:

- professional identity – where professionals are socialised into similar values and perceptions and so have a limited understanding of other professions;
- the relative status of different professions – where there are perceived status differentials between professions;

- professional discretion and accountability – there may be differences in individual discretion and autonomy between different professions.

Other commentators (Kharicha et al, 2005; Reed et al, 2005; Lymbery, 2006) have reflected on similar difficulties for staff working across different professions. Kharicha et al (2005) and Lymbery (2006) both cite Huntington, whose work, published in 1981, highlighted the differences in general practitioners' (GPs') and social workers' professional cultures. Some of these differences include:

- a reliance on the medical model by doctors, which social workers (who subscribe to a social model of health) see as too restrictive and focused on people's functional inabilities (Bywaters, 1986, cited in Lymbery, 2006);
- an 'action versus holding orientation' (Huntington, 1981, cited in Kharicha, 2005, p 404) whereby doctors are trained to make swift decisions to respond to emergency situations whereas social workers are trained to make a decision after all options have been explored;
- a status and power for doctors that has been long established and is not shared by the social work profession (Huntington, 1981, cited in Kharicha et al, 2005; Manthorpe and Iliffe, 2003; Lymbery, 2006).

However, despite the difficulties, the findings from evaluations of pilot projects of social workers attached to, or located within, GPs' surgeries have been largely positive, reporting improved communication between workers, more appropriate referrals to social workers and speedy response rates (for a summary of these studies, see Glasby and Littlechild, 2004, pp 130–5). More recently, Kharicha et al (2005) undertook a study on the perspectives of social workers and GPs in two locations in London. In summary they found:

- Social workers and GPs agreed on the need for joint working but each profession wanted the other to change its way of working.
- Co-location was seen as desirable for improved communication but a possible threat to social workers because of concerns about isolation and about differences in power and hierarchical authority.
- Ways of resolving conflict identified by social workers included minimising risk, adopting pragmatic, case-specific solutions (not always consistent with policy), using nurses as mediators between themselves and doctors and resorting to the authority of their managers.
- The availability of resources and professional skills may be more important than organisational arrangements, such as co-location or integrated teams, in working collaboratively.

While much of the evidence above comes under what Hudson (2002, p 9) would call the 'pessimistic tradition' of interprofessionality, he identifies more encouraging evidence with professionals working together on a project in Sedgefield, which adopts a whole systems approach to service delivery and change (Hudson, 2005). The project has brought together workers from social care, community nursing and housing to deliver services to older people and physically disabled adults. The evaluation has been positive from the perspectives of staff and service users, identifying improved ways of working including:

- greater understanding of the roles and responsibilities of other team members and a parity of esteem between them all;
- responding more quickly and more creatively to problems;
- being flexible in relation to professional boundaries.

While the project has not been without difficulties, many of which have stemmed from barriers imposed by central government, Hudson advocates a new, more 'optimistic' model of interprofessional working based on the following hypotheses:

- That members of one profession may have more in common with members of a different profession than their own.
- That the promotion of professional values to service users can form the basis of inter-professional partnership.
- That association to an immediate work group can override professional or hierarchical differences among staff (Hudson, 2005, p 2).

Outcomes for older people

Regardless of whether or not the process of integrated working works smoothly or not, the acid test is whether older people and their carers experience improved services as a result of partnership working, and here the evidence is inconclusive at best (SCIE, 2006). Reed et al (2005) examined the available literature on how strategies, including the development of posts such as care coordinators and liaison nurses to help older people negotiate the complex array of relevant services, have improved outcomes for older people and their carers. While they claim that there is a vast literature *describing* how these roles have been developed to address difficulties of communication and coordination, they conclude that the evidence on their effectiveness for improving services to older people and their carers is equivocal.

Kharicha et al (2004), in reviewing outcomes for older people of collaborative working between health and social care professionals, identified only five relevant studies, none of which demonstrated significant evidence of beneficial outcomes. Similar conclusions were made by Brown et al (2002, 2003) in their comparison of outcomes for older people from integrated health–social care teams and traditional social work teams in Wiltshire.

Recent research funded by the Department of Health concluded that, overall, partnership working between health and social care agencies did produce outcomes which service users and carers valued (Modernising Adult Social Care Research Initiative, 2007). In particular, a study by the University of Glasgow of 15 sites where partnership working was in place concluded that operational features which produced positive outcomes for adult service users included:

- co-location of staff, providing a single point of contact;
- organisation of staff into multidisciplinary teams to provide holistic care;
- specialist partnership dedicated to particular user groups;
- partnerships extending beyond social care and health to allow access to a range of services to promote well-being (Miller and Cook, 2007; Modernising Adult Social Care Research Initiative, 2007).

What does this mean for practice?

Drawing on the narrative accounts of 57 social work practitioners, service users and carers, Cree and Davis (2007) conclude that despite the changes and uncertainty currently inherent in social work, the essential qualities of a social worker remain the same: 'their ability to listen to people, to advocate on behalf of others and see them in the context of their whole lives' (p 12). In a similar vein, Lymbery (2006, p 1129) identifies unique characteristics that social workers with older people can bring to multidisciplinary teams based on their commitment to anti-oppressive values and their orientation to practice. These include:

- the ability to form positive relationships with older people;
- an emphasis on the older person at the centre of the assessment process;
- a commitment to undertaking an assessment at the pace of the older person;
- the ability to understand people within the wider context of their families and communities;
- an ability to work effectively within networks and organisations;
- particular skills in coordinating care packages.

The narrative accounts presented in Practice Examples 1 and 2 from two hospital social workers show how these kinds of skills can be used to undertake effective partnership working with colleagues and with older people and their carers.

Practice Example 1

Julie

'Miss A is a 90-year-old woman who was admitted to hospital with a urinary tract infection – she was walking a little but was confused. She lives alone, has regular support from her niece and nephew, both in their 70s, who go round daily, provide food and ensure her six cats are fed regularly. She had never had any support from social services. Once she got to hospital, she refused to speak to any of the hospital staff or me, she was asleep each time I saw her and often fell asleep at meal times. Still, her condition improved to the extent that the consultant declared her medically fit for discharge. However, from the description of her lifestyle given by her family, her physical condition when she was admitted and her nephew's reluctance to continue to support her if she was discharged home, the consultant declared that she would be too much of a risk living at home alone and said that she couldn't make that decision for herself.

Anyway, I felt that Miss A hadn't really been given a chance. I couldn't get her to speak to me, so I spoke to the niece and explained that the consultant wanted us to find a nursing home place for her aunt. She in turn spoke to her aunt and explained my role. It turns out that Miss A had never been in hospital in the 90 years of her life! She was terrified! She couldn't cope with the rules and saw the OTs [occupational therapists] and physios [physiotherapists] as "doers", not as people to talk to. She said, "I know what I'm doing, I want to go home".

Once she'd said that, I knew what I'd got to do. At the multidisciplinary case conference, all the medical staff insisted she couldn't go home. I stuck out on my own and got the consultant to agree to review her medication. Nobody was happy but they reluctantly agreed.

At last she went home with a hoist and two carers going in four times a day to support her. She had a pendant alarm in case she fell. After a bit she said, "I'm not having this, being hoisted around all the time." We found she got herself out to the conservatory to find her zimmerframe, using the trolley the OTs had supplied!

I went back to the ward and told them how she was. That's really important, keeping them informed – when you've had a few successes you feel a bit more confident!'

In this account of her work with Miss A, Julie demonstrates the importance of social workers acting as *advocates* on behalf of older people who may not be able to get their voices heard by other professionals. In some cases this can bring you into conflict with colleagues and require you to exercise careful *negotiation skills*. As this account shows, the importance of *good communication and feedback* cannot be underestimated.

Practice Example 2

George

'Recently I was called to carry out an assessment with Mr B who had been admitted with a deterioration in his multiple sclerosis but was now said by the doctor to be "fit for discharge". A case conference had been called by the OT involving herself, a physio, consultant, nurse and family members. I was given one day's notice but I managed to contact family members and introduce myself over the phone and explain my role. I didn't have time to contact anyone else. I arrived on the ward, met members of the family and the conference commenced. Sadly within minutes of the meeting starting it becomes clear that I am not going to be "flavour of the month". Mrs B and family had been given a totally misleading picture of what I could and could not provide for her husband. For example, the OT and physio had painted a "wonderful" picture that we could provide three or even four calls per day whenever Mr B or his wife wanted! We could also provide a sitting service every night if they wanted this, meals on wheels, respite care, etc, etc … and yes … it is all true! BUT … at this point I need to explain to them the cost. Then I have to explain there may be a delay, and services as outlined above are not always readily on tap, very often there is a waiting list. And then I remind myself of the Value Requirement from my training course – "To promote people's right to choice, privacy, confidentiality etc … while recognising and addressing the complexities of competing rights and demands". Complexities and demands are indeed key words here!

The problem here is false expectations have been given by other professionals who do not have to pay for it, don't know the availability of resources, and also don't know the correct procedures to obtain such services. Clearly, I have been undermined.

Of course, there is little value in my pointing all this out and apportioning blame at the meeting. I instead chose to start on a positive and say "Yes, such services can be provided" before introducing my "however". I did my best to lower the expectations that had previously been raised in my absence and apologised for the way they had to some extent been misled.

Following the meeting, where a plan was agreed upon, albeit with a large dose of "compromise", I requested to meet with the OT and physio in private. We discussed the situation and they were genuinely surprised at the lack of resources available and the high demand for them, which in turn surprised *me*! And yet, they were rather young practitioners and fairly new to that hospital.

In the end, we agreed that there had been a "misunderstanding" and I wanted to start afresh ... and we did ... bridges were built. Unfortunately, Mr B was in hospital a further week before resources were available for him to return home. Social services were not seen as the "wicked witch of the west" but they were not seen as "fairy godmother" either!

All because of lack of communication, education and of sharing information, at the right time, in the right place, and by the right people!'

In this account of his work with Mr B, George demonstrates how investment in *understanding the roles and responsibilities* of other professionals is crucial to effective partnership working. The initial failure to do so in this situation could have had negative consequences for Mr B and affected future working relationships between George and his colleagues. *Establishing realistic expectations* on the part of older people, their carers and all professionals involved in the situation is a sound basis for effective partnership working.

Practice learning points

Other authors have devised comprehensive lists of key principles for effective interprofessional partnership working (see, for example, Barrett et al, 2005, p 18; Carnwell and Buchanan, 2005, p 272). On the basis of the two narratives above, this chapter similarly concludes with a number of practice learning points that will be useful for *any* social worker for older people who wants to work effectively in partnership, regardless of the setting in which they work.

(1) Be clear about and have confidence in your own knowledge and skills. As a social worker you do have important and different perspectives and skills to offer. Julie and George both showed that they worked most effectively *alongside* other professionals – neither of them professed to be able to provide an effective service on their own but were able to complement the contributions of other professionals.

(2) Social work puts principles of empowerment and anti-discriminatory practice at the heart of its value base. You may expect that you will take a broader, more holistic approach to assessment that takes more account of wider family and societal pressures than will other professionals. Miss A saw the social worker as having a less functional view of her situation than did the physiotherapists and occupational therapists and so was able to talk to her more easily.

(3) Taking a person-centred approach to the assessment process will mean that you act as an advocate for some older people who have difficulty having their voices heard. This may mean that you are at odds with the other professionals, as was Julie in relation to Miss A. This may not always feel comfortable but as you develop confidence and trust in other professionals, you are more likely to establish effective working relations.

(4) Undertaking a holistic assessment of an older person involves establishing a relationship with them and that takes time. This approach is sometimes in conflict with the administratively driven model of care management that is currently dominant. Had Julie not taken time to understand Miss A and explore further the situation she was in, Miss A would have been admitted to a residential home directly from hospital.

(5) Always try to put yourself in the place of the older person and their carers with whom you are working. If they are involved with you as a social worker, they are likely to be feeling unwell or at a point of crisis in their lives. They may well be confused about the number and range of professionals whom they are meeting and what they all do.

Be honest and straightforward and try and help people understand what is going on.

(6) Good communication was the key to effective partnership working in the situations described above. When you know that new colleagues are arriving whom you are likely to be working with, take time to let them know about your job and find out what they do. Had George and his colleagues communicated about their respective roles earlier, they would not have found themselves in potential conflict when discussing the future care of Mr B.

(7) Keep updated about differing priorities and available resources and inform other colleagues about them. Had George done this with his occupational and physiotherapy colleagues the unrealistic expectations that Mr and Mrs B had would not have occurred.

(8) If conflict does arise, make sure you deal with disagreements with colleagues away from the older person and their family. George clarified the situation about resources with Mr and Mrs B without blaming his colleagues and simply arranged to see them in private later where he could explain the policy and procedures that governed his actions.

(9) Maintain an openness of mind to develop an understanding of and trust in the expertise and skill of other professionals. Too often workers approach joint working with stereotypes and preconceptions of how other professionals will behave. This can often have detrimental effects on the person with whom you are working.

(10) Get to know other key people in the community and what resources and strengths they bring. You can meet other professionals, voluntary groups and volunteers by setting up informal bi-monthly meetings, varying the venue and ensuring that everyone has the opportunity to put faces to names.

(11) Don't forget the importance of giving feedback to other professionals involved about what the outcome has been for older people with whom they've worked. When Julie informed the nursing staff about how Miss A had successfully settled back in the community, she was not only giving them important feedback on Miss A but establishing further her credibility as a trustworthy colleague whose judgements could be trusted.

(12) Celebrate your successes together! Success leads to better morale for staff and helps create an atmosphere of trust and confidence for the future.

Conclusion

While the legislative and policy framework for the delivery of services to older people is constantly changing, a number of themes remain the same:

- While the emphasis now is on social inclusion, preventive services and earlier intervention, partnership working between agencies continues to be seen as a positive means of achieving these aims.
- The current government seems unlikely to make any major structural reforms in the relationships between key public sector agencies, therefore many of the organisational barriers to partnership working will remain unresolved.
- In all the government guidelines, advice on how to implement partnership working remains at such a level of generality that many different models are emerging. However, as Hudson concludes, 'there is now a sharper understanding of the inescapable need for working across a system ... and a growing understanding of how the process can be undertaken ... Doing nothing is not an option' (Hudson, 2006, p 21).

Evidence from research and practice cited above demonstrates that joint working is complex. Members of different professions come from different perspectives, have different knowledge and skills, and different perceptions of status and autonomy. However, the evidence also shows that with vision, trust, commitment and a conducive organisational environment, partnership working can be effective. Nevertheless, much of the research to date has been on understanding problems and implementing strategies to address them without having firm evidence of what improvements they make to the lives of older people and their carers. The focus of research and future service development must now firmly be on what forms of partnership improve outcomes for older people and what helps more people see 'the whole picture on the box' (quoted in Hudson, 2006, p 5).

Trigger questions

➲ Why might older people react differently to different professionals?

➲ How can you best communicate your own role and skills to other colleagues?

➲ How can you extend effective joint working beyond the people you work alongside?

Recommended resources

➲ The *International Journal of Integrated Care* is a free online journal with articles from different countries focused on all aspects of integrated care, www.ijic.org

➲ The UK Centre for the Advancement of Interprofessional Education (CAIPE) is a national organisation that promotes teaching and education that helps workers from different backgrounds and settings to learn from and with each other, www.caipe.org.uk

➲ Age Concern England (www.ace.org.uk) and Help the Aged (www.helptheaged.org.uk) are two key voluntary organisations that have policy briefings and up-to-date information available in accessible language on their websites.

➲ Carers UK represents the voices of people providing unpaid care by looking after an ill, frail or disabled family member, friend or partner. Their website is a source of information on policy, campaigns and resources, www.carersuk.org

References

Audit Commission (1986) *Making a Reality of Community Care*, London: HMSO.

Audit Commission (2002) *Integrated Services for Older People: Building a Whole System Approach in England*, London: Audit Commission.

Barrett, G., Sellman, D. and Thomas, J. (2005) *Interprofessional Working in Health and Social Care*, Basingstoke: Palgrave.

Brown, L., Tucker, C. and Domokos, T. (2002) *The Impact of Integrated Health and Social Care Teams on Older People Living in the Community*, Bath: University of Bath.

Brown, L., Tucker, C. and Domokos, T. (2003) 'Evaluating the impact of integrated health and social care teams on older people living in the community', *Health and Social Care in the Community*, vol 11, no 2, pp 85-94.

Bywaters, P. (1986) 'Social work and the medical profession: arguments against unconditional collaboration', *British Journal of Social Work*, vol 16, no 6, pp 661-77.

Carnwell, R. and Buchanan, J. (2005) *Effective Practice in Health and Social Care: A Partnership Approach*, Maidenhead: Open University.

Challis, D., Stewart, K., Donnelly, M., Weiner, K. and Hughes, J. (2006) 'Care management for older people: does integration make a difference?', *Journal of Interprofessional Care*, vol 20, no 4, pp 335-48.

Cree, V. and Davis, A (2007) *Social Work, Voices from the Inside*, Abingdon: Routledge.

DH (Department of Health) (1998) *Modernising Social Services: Promoting Independence, Improving Protection, Raising Standards*, London: The Stationery Office.

DH (2000) *The NHS Plan: A Plan for Investment, A Plan for Reform*, London: The Stationery Office.

DH (2001) *National Service Framework for Older People: Modern Standards and Service Models*, London: DH.

DH (2006a) *Our Health, Our Care, Our Say: A New Direction for Community Services*, Cmd 6737, London: DH.

DH (2006b) 'More older people to be given choice to live at home', Press Release, 2006/0103, London: DH.

Dowling, B., Powell, M. and Glendinning, C. (2004) 'Conceptualising successful partnerships', *Health and Social Care in the Community*, vol 12, no 4, pp 309-17.

Glasby, J. and Littlechild, R. (2004) *The Health and Social Care Divide: The Experiences of Older People*, Bristol: The Policy Press.

Glasby, J. and Peck, E. (2003) *Care Trusts: Partnership Working in Action*, Oxford: Radcliffe Medical Press.

Glendinning, C., Hudson, B., Hardy, B. and Young, R. (2002) *National Evaluation of Notifications for the use of the Section 31 Partnership Flexibilities in the Health Act 1999: Final Project Report*, Leeds/Manchester, Nuffield Institute of Health/National Primary Care Research and Development Centre.

GSCC (General Social Care Council) (2002) *Codes of Practice for Social Care Workers and Employers*, London: GSCC.

HM Government (2005) *Opportunity Age: Meeting the Challenges of Ageing in the 21st Century*, London: The Stationery Office.

Hudson, B. (2002) 'Interprofessionality in health and social care: the Achilles' heel of partnerships?', *Journal of Interprofessional Care*, vol 16, pp 199-210.

Hudson, B. (2005) 'Grounds for optimism', *Community Care*, 1 December, www.communitycare.co.uk/Articles/2005/12/01/51988/Grounds+for+optimism

Hudson, B. (2006) *Whole Systems Working: A Guide and Discussion Paper*, Care Services Improvement Agency/Integrated Care Network, www.icn.csip.org.uk

Huntington, J. (1981) *Social Work and General Medical Practice*, London: George Allen and Unwin.

Kharicha, K., Illiffe, S., Levin, E., Davey, B. and Fleming, C. (2005) 'Tearing down the Berlin wall: social workers' perspectives on joint working with general practice', *Family Practice*, vol 22, no 4, pp 399-405.

Kharicha, K., Levin, E., Illiffe, S. and Davey, B. (2004) 'Social work, general practice and evidence-based policy in the collaborative care of older people: current problems and future possibilities', *Health and Social Care in the Community*, vol 12, no 2, pp 134-41.

Lymbery, M. (2006) 'United we stand? Partnership working in health and social care and the role of social work in services for older people', *British Journal of Social Work*, vol 36, pp 1119-34.

Manthorpe, J. and Iliffe, S. (2003) 'Professional predictions: June Huntington's perspectives on joint working, 20 years on', *Interprofessional Social Work*, vol 17, no 1, pp 85-94.

Means, R., Morbey, H. and Smith, R. (2002) *From Community Care to Market Care? The Development of Welfare Services for Older People*, Bristol: The Policy Press.

Miller, E. and Cook, A. (2007) *Users and Carers Define Effective Partnerships in Health and Social Care*, Edinburgh: Scottish Executive Joint Improvement Team, www.jitscotland.org.uk/

Modernising Adult Social Care Research Initiative (2007) *Modernising Adult Social Care – What's Working*, London: DH.

ODPM (Office of the Deputy Prime Minister) (2006) *A Sure Start to Later Life: Ending Inequalities for Older People*, London: ODPM.

Parrott, L. (2006) *Values and Ethics in Social Work Practice*, Exeter: Learning Matters.

Postle, K. (2002) 'Working between the idea and the reality: ambiguities and tensions in case managers' work', *British Journal of Social Work*, vol 32, no 3, pp 335-52.

Quality Assurance Agency for Higher Education (2000) *Benchmark Statement for Social Policy and Social Work*, Gloucester: QAA.

Reed, J., Cook, G., Childs, S. and McCormack, B. (2005) 'A literature review to explore integrated care for older people', *International Journal of Integrated Care*, vol 5, www.ijic.org

SCIE (Social Care Institute for Excellence) (2006) *Outcomes-focused Services for Older People*, London: SCIE, www.scie.org.uk

TOPSS (2002) *National Occupational Standards for Social Work*, London: TOPSS.

Whittington, C. (2003) 'Collaboration and partnership in context', in J. Weinstein, C. Whittington and T. Leiba (eds) *Collaboration in Social Work Practice*, London: Jessica Kingsley.

Conclusion

Kate Morris

This book has focused on multi-agency working as a context for social work learning and practice in England. It is not feasible to draw out overarching messages about multi-agency working from international literature – the diversity in contexts and purposes for practice render this an unproductive exercise. The evidence in, for example, child welfare suggests that developments elsewhere may have a more uneven interest in multi-agency working than is currently demonstrated in the UK. In other areas of social care practice, international emphasis varies from integrated practice through to multiple funding streams. However, the commonality of messages emerging from the UK experience offers useful insights for developing practice.

As the preceding chapters have described, the legal and policy expectations for multi-agency working are embedded within the frameworks for practice for much of current UK social care provision. This has resulted in contributors describing a range of approaches and practice issues for social work. Within this there are some common emerging themes; these themes can be identified as:

- understandings for practice;
- the impact of multi-agency working on outcomes;
- how service users influence arrangements for multi-agency working.

Understandings for practice

Using the contributions in this text it is possible to arrive at the following understandings of the different terms being used to describe the arrangements for several agencies coming together to deliver services:

- *Multi-agency working* – this captures the arrangements and processes for a number of single agencies to come together to plan and deliver services that have shared aims and outcomes. These may be services at an individual level or at a community level. It does not necessarily indicate the pooling of budgets, the co-location of staff, the merging of services or the sharing of management functions. There are examples of this in the chapters by Coad, Galvani and Littlechild (Chapters Three, Seven and Nine) and contributors appear to suggest a sub-categorisation of 'joint working' where two agencies come together to co-deliver a service.

■ *Collaborative working* – this describes the sharing of professional responsibilities to deliver a service with mutually agreed outcomes. This may indicate the co-location of staff, the pooling of budgets and the merging of organisational structures and arrangements. The chapters by Hughes and Prior, Edwards et al and Galvani (Chapters Two, Four and Seven) contain such examples.

■ *Partnership working* – this term is used somewhat loosely in the contributing chapters. It appears to have two descriptive functions: to describe the relationship between the professional and the service user (as used by Jordan and Ward, Chapters Five and Eight) and to describe the overall governance arrangements for services (as used by Hughes and Prior, Chapter Two). This difference in use in part reflects the different histories for the service areas. Partnership working came to the fore in child welfare with the introduction of the 1989 Children Act and was concerned with the working relationship between professionals and children and families (Tunnard, 1991). For adult care services the emerging arrangements for local and national governance for service provision and development was the focus of concerns about partnership working (Glendinning et al, 2002). This differing use of the same term highlights the potential for complexity in communication and dialogue when holistic services are being developed.

For each set of terms there are self-evident implications for practice; the extent to which single services become merged, as opposed to simply sharing desired outcomes, has significant ramifications for the learning needs and professional identities of the social work practitioners involved. This grouping of the contributors' use of the terms presents a means by which to consider the arrangements being described and their consequences for practice. However, of equal, if not more, importance is the diversity in usage. The contributors repeatedly point to the need for a shared language and common understandings – themes reflected in much of the literature surrounding multi-agency working (Dowling et al, 2004). However, there does not appear to be a common language being used in multi-agency working. As a result of the absence of commonly agreed terms to describe the activity being considered, early groundwork is necessary if clarity of purpose and process is to be arrived at. Specifically, those developing multi-agency working at strategic and practice levels will need to arrive at a shared language to describe their work – and within this will need to be common understandings of the intended outcomes.

As Barnes et al (2005) suggest, one of the values of multi-agency working is the capacity for such arrangements to support extended understandings of the needs being responded to and the activity being developed. They propose that effective multi-agency working includes a collective move towards enhanced understandings, and that if the process of drawing together multi-agency arrangements simply rests on individual stakeholders signing up to pre-existing understandings of the problems/responses then the benefits from shared working are diluted.

Throughout this text, and elsewhere, there is a repeated emphasis on the importance of arriving at shared, articulated statements of intended outcomes. The absence of such frameworks is described as a key barrier to effective multi-agency working. For social workers this suggests a number of messages for practice. These include:

- having clarity about the role and remit of social work in any specific service setting – the qualifying frameworks stress the value and need for social workers to be clear about their roles and responsibilities. As Edwards et al (2006) suggest, effective multi-agency working is not the dilution of skills into a generic care practitioner – instead it is recognising and drawing on expertise held by each contributing professional;
- enabling the process of arriving at shared agreements and language – if, as Frost et al (2005) suggest, social work is the key to effective multi-agency working, facilitating the process of arriving at a shared understanding of purpose would seem an appropriate social work activity.

The impact of multi-agency working on outcomes

Several contributors to this text describe the paucity of evidence about the impact of multi-agency working on outcomes for those using services. Galvani suggests in Chapter Seven that little is known about the outcomes and impact of multi-agency drugs and substance use teams for those with dependency problems, and Littlechild (Chapter Nine) argues that:

> While there is a growing body of published literature about partnership working at a strategic and an organisational level and in relation to interprofessional working, there is little evidence yet about the effects of partnership working on the lives of older people and their carers.

The contributors indicate that evidence centres on the structures and processes being developed for multi-agency working, rather than service user impact and outcomes. These reflections are echoed elsewhere. The large-scale evaluations of national partnership-based initiatives such as the Children's Fund also suggest an emphasis on process rather than outcomes (Edwards et al, 2006). While the evaluation of the Children's Fund was able to identify some models of multi-agency working, its relatively short-term nature prevented the longitudinal study of the impact of joined-up strategies and provision on outcomes for children and families. Likewise, Frost et al (2005) note that they are able to explore the dynamics of social work practice within a number of multidisciplinary teams, but outcome data for those using the services is limited. In adult services, as Ward suggests, learning from the experiences of those using the services may well be key to their efficacy but research focused on outcomes is still embryonic.

The drive towards multi-agency working seems at first glance, Balloch suggests, to 'make a lot of sense' (Balloch and Taylor, 2001, p 1). The complexity of its development and implementation has generated a wealth of research. Nevertheless, as Sloper (2004) and Abbott (2005) reveal, concerns to improve the internal dynamics of multi-agency teams may not result in changes in the impact of the service on need or outcomes. The study by Townsley et al (2004) of multi-agency services for children with complex needs does indicate that professionals experienced this approach as a positive development. However, despite positive responses by families there was also evidence that the families still faced significant and enduring difficulties.

Multi-agency working may not alone be sufficient to achieve the changes needed for those using the services – again a finding echoed in the large-scale evaluations of the initiatives that supported local partnership working. This is an important debate, and one that links to the role of those using the services in influencing provision. Sloper (2004, p 571) argues the need for robust, methodologically sound research that 'explores the ways in which the factors identified as facilitating multi-agency working relate to outcomes'.

Exploring outcomes is methodologically and ethically challenging (see, for example, Hanson and Plewis, 2004; Hughes and Fielding, 2006). The use of large-scale datasets may not capture the nuances of individual child- and/or adult-level experiences; likewise the emphasis on small-scale qualitative research may not generate the impact data that is needed for outcomes to be established. It is difficult to attribute specific outcomes to certain characteristics of service delivery – particularly in settings where multiple providers have joined together. This is not to negate the positive commentary from some service users, but instead suggests that further research is needed. The move towards outcome-based social care activity (see, for example, the *Every Child Matters* guidance: DfES, 2004; the *Youth Matters* Green Paper: DfES, 2006; and the emerging policy work by the Social Exclusion Unit exploring adult exclusion: SEU, 2007) means that the linking of process and system data with an analysis of the impact of the multi-agency arrangements is set to become an increasing priority for practitioners and policy makers.

How service users influence arrangements for multi-agency working

As Jordan explores in Chapter Five, families are able to articulate what they see as helpful and unhelpful approaches to addressing their needs. This is a message a number of the contributors echo. In Chapter Three Coad describes the current emphasis within child health and social care on exploring the involvement of children in service planning – but she also identifies the challenges and barriers to effective practice in this area. (Spicer and Evans, 2006, suggest that for children and young people, even when the surrounding context promotes participation, the reality is that extended consultation or service evaluation tends to be the focus of involvement.)

Throughout this text the extent and nature of the involvement of those using social care services provided in multi-agency settings has been questioned. In some areas there is little, if any, evidence of active participation. Hughes and Prior in Chapter Two and Galvani in Chapter Seven indicate limited service user involvement in the design and delivery of youth justice provision or drug and alcohol services – reflecting the complex debates that exist about rights and responsibilities and participation: the extent to which active participation in developing multi-agency provision is accepted is linked to debates about legitimacy and citizenship (Burford, 2005). For many families and adults facing enduring and multiple difficulties, participating in the development of services is rare (Morris et al, 2007). Complex debates surround participative practice for those families seen to be 'undeserving' of engagement (Merkel-Holguin, 2004). These ethical and moral dilemmas are no less reflected in the context of multi-agency working than they are in any other social care setting.

What is clear from the contributors is that there is still considerable learning necessary for professionals to be able to ensure that service users play a full role in multi-agency working. Adult and children's services do hold examples of participative initiatives that have sought to enable service user expertise to be influential in the services received; however, there are particular challenges for the participation of service users when professionals are themselves unclear as to their roles and influence (Morris, 2004). This lack of clarity about social work within multi-agency settings is set against a backdrop of some complexity for social work in arriving at full understandings of participation and partnership (Jackson and Morris, 1994; Levin, 2004).

For social work practice the messages in this text are:

- The participation of those using the services is both a requirement and a necessary development for effective outcomes in multi-agency working.

- The skills that social work has built into advocacy and empowerment have an important role in supporting and promoting participation in multi-agency working – where other professionals may be exposed to this dimension of practice for the first time.
- Social work will have a particular role – given its knowledge base and emphasis – in ensuring that service users are represented in the development of multi-agency services.
- Marginalised and excluded groups and communities face particular barriers to accessing and taking up services. Social work's commitment to inclusion and anti-oppressive practice means that social work will be seen to hold specific responsibilities for ensuring representation and participation for all those needing social care services.

Concluding comments

Williams (2002) suggests that it is developing the skills of professionals to cross traditional boundaries (he refers to the idea of a 'competent boundary spanner') and fulfil key roles in negotiating inter-agency relationships that is a crucial ingredient in effective multi-agency working. This focus on the role of the individual is, he argues, less well developed than the focus on strategic and operational management arrangements. National Evaluation of the Children's Fund (NECF) (2004) also point to the pivotal role specific individuals play in supporting joint working. However, they also argue that too much emphasis can be placed on what they call the 'hero practitioner' at the expense of broader change in structures and processes. Frost et al (2005) argue that social work is *the* key interdisciplinary profession – and serves often as the glue or cement in multi-agency working arrangements. Within this text there are repeated messages about the importance of social work practitioners in enabling the joining up of services. As this chapter has suggested, such an emphasis may not always be helpful; social work may not be the appropriate change agent, service users may get lost in the focus on professional matters and more evidence is needed to unpack the links between outcomes and professional inter-agency arrangements. Nevertheless, contributors to this text are able to articulate the core skills social workers need to practise in a legal and policy framework that repeatedly reinforces the need for multi-agency working.

The picture presented suggests that social work cannot simply be 'bolted on' to existing provision – an experience echoed in various evaluations exploring the integration of health and social care services (see, for example, Glasby and Peck, 2003). The emergence of new dedicated services, like those described by Hughes and Prior in Chapter Two, may allow professionals to negotiate shared new approaches that draw on a range of skills and knowledge. However, for many multi-agency settings the experience of developing multi-agency working can be seen to be one of territorial debates and difficulties.

The value of multi-agency working lies in being able to respond holistically to needs and arriving at broader understandings of causes and possible responses. The message for social work practitioners emerging from the learning within the range of services described in this text is the value of ensuring that multi-agency working goes beyond narrow pre-existing understandings. Instead, being able to integrate the knowledge and perspectives of all those contributing to the service, and finding processes for being able to arrive at collective approaches that draw on the different resources, are crucial.

While individual practitioners cannot alone resolve strategic dilemmas there are messages within this book about the value of social workers reflecting upon the histories of those coming together to deliver services, and using their skills of facilitation, negotiation and innovation to enable these pre-histories to be ameliorated.

References

Abbott, D. (2005) 'Multi-agency working in services for disabled children: what impact does it have on professionals?', *Health and Social Care in the Community*, vol 13, no 2, pp 155-63.

Balloch, S. and Taylor, M. (eds) (2001) *Partnership Working: Policy and Practice*, Bristol: The Policy Press.

Barnes, M., Mason, P. and Edwards, A. (2005) *The National Evaluation of the Children's Fund: Interim Thematic Report*, London: NECF/DfES.

DfES (Department for Education and Skills) (2004) *Every Child Matters: Change for Children*, London: DfES.

DfES (2006) *Youth Matters: Next Steps*, London: DfES.

Dowling, B., Powell, M. and Glendinning, C. (2004) 'Conceptualising successful partnerships', *Health & Social Care in the Community*, vol 12, no 4, pp 309-17.

Edwards, A., Barnes, M., Plewis, I. and Morris, K. (2006) *The National Evaluation of the Children's Fund Final Report*, London: DfES.

Frost, N., Robinson, M. and Anning, A. (2005) 'Social workers in multi disciplinary teams: issues and dilemmas for professional practice', *Child and Family Social Work*, vol 10, pp 187-96.

Glasby, J. and Peck, E. (eds) (2003) *Care Trusts: Partnership Working In Action*, Oxford: Radcliffe Medical Press.

Glendinning, C., Powell, M. and Rummery, K. (eds) (2002) *Partnerships, New Labour and the Governance of Welfare*, Bristol: The Policy Press.

Hansen, K. and Plewis, I. (2004) *Children at Risk: How Evidence from British Cohort Data can Inform the Debate on Prevention*, NECF, www.ne-cf.org

Hughes, N. and Fielding, A. (2006) *Targeting Preventative Services for Children: Experiences from the Children's Fund*, London: DfES.

Jackson, S. and Morris, K. (1994) *Looking at Partnership Teaching in Social Work Qualifying Programmes*, London: CCETSW.

Levin, E. (2004) *Involving Service Users and Carers in Social Work Education*, London: Social Care Institute for Excellence.

Merkel-Holguin, L. (2004) 'Sharing power with the people: family group conferencing as a democratic experiment', *Journal of Sociology & Social Welfare*, vol 31, no 1, pp 155-73.

Morris, K. (2004) 'Partnership working: changing understandings in child welfare services in England', *Protecting Children*, vol 19, no 2, pp 130-41.

Morris, K., Hughes, N., Clarke, H., Tew, J., Mason, P., Galvani, S., Lewis, P., Becker, S., Burford, G. and Loveless, L. (2007) *Whole Family Approaches: A Review of the Literature*, London: SEU.

NECF (National Evaluation of the Children's Fund) (2004) *Multi-agency Working for Prevention for Children and Families*, www.ne-cf.org

SEU (Social Exclusion Unit) (2007) *Reaching Out: Think Family*, London: SEU.

Sloper, P. (2004) 'Facilitators and barriers for co-ordinated multi-agency services', *Child Care Health and Development*, vol 6, pp 571-80.

Spicer, N. and Evans, R. (2006) 'Developing children and young people's participation in strategic processes', *Social Policy and Society*, vol 5, no 2, pp 177-88.

Townsley, R., Abbott, D. and Watson, D. (2004) *Making a Difference? Exploring the Impact of Multi-agency Working on Disabled Children with Complex Health Care Needs, their Families and the Professionals who Support Them*, Bristol: The Policy Press.

Tunnard, J. (1991) *The Children Act 1989: Working in Partnership with Families*, London: Family Rights Group/HMSO.

Williams, P. (2002) 'The competent boundary spanner', *Public Administration*, vol 80, no 1, pp 103-24.

Index